"You Know That You're Driving Me Insane, Don't You?"

"I'm sorry." The liquid look in her eyes denied her contrite words. Noel was thrilled that she was able to arouse that escalating, desperate hunger in him. The slight trembling of his hand stroking her fingertips only proved, without a doubt, that Ross was as affected by those same strong forces which had been buffeting her about with all the power of a hurricane. He might be far more experienced in such matters than she, but he wasn't a good enough actor to fake such responses.

JOANN ROBBINS

is an incurable optimist and romantic at heart and she believes steadfastly in happy endings, which is why she enjoys writing romance novels. She lives in Arizona with her husband and teenage son, both of whom she fell in love with at first sight.

Dear Reader:

SILHOUETTE DESIRE is an exciting new line of contemporary romances from Silhouette Books. During the past year, many Silhouette readers have written in telling us what other types of stories they'd like to read from Silhouette, and we've kept these comments and suggestions in mind in developing SILHOUETTE DESIRE.

DESIREs feature all of the elements you like to see in a romance, plus a more sensual, provocative story. So if you want to experience all the excitement, passion and joy of falling in love, then SILHOUETTE DESIRE is for you.

I hope you enjoy this book and all the wonderful stories to come from SILHOUETTE DESIRE. I'd appreciate any thoughts you'd like to share with us on new SILHOUETTE DESIRE, and I invite you to write to us at the address below:

> Karen Solem
> Editor-in-Chief
> Silhouette Books
> P.O. Box 769
> New York, N.Y. 10019

JOANN ROBBINS
Winning Season

Silhouette Desire
Published by Silhouette Books New York
America's Publisher of Contemporary Romance

SILHOUETTE BOOKS, a Division of Simon & Schuster, Inc.
1230 Avenue of the Americas, New York, N.Y. 10020

Copyright © 1983 by JoAnn Robbins

Distributed by Pocket Books

All rights reserved, including the right to reproduce
this book or portions thereof in any form whatsoever.
For information address Silhouette Books, 1230
Avenue of the Americas, New York, N.Y. 10020

ISBN: 0-671-49378-1

First Silhouette Books printing October, 1983

10 9 8 7 6 5 4 3 2 1

All of the characters in this book are fictitious. Any resemblance to actual persons, living or dead, is purely coincidental.

SILHOUETTE, SILHOUETTE DESIRE and colophon are registered trademarks of Simon & Schuster, Inc.

America's Publisher of Contemporary Romance

Printed in the U.S.A.

Winning Season

1

"Jeff, I won't do it!"

Noel Heywood slammed her blue earthenware coffee mug down onto the desk with enough force to send splatters of the dark liquid spraying across the slim skirt of her cream-colored suit.

Darn, she thought, that's just great. Now I'll have to change before air time! She reached for a tissue and began dabbing furiously at the spreading dark stain, irritation creasing her forehead.

"Noel, you haven't even let me finish!" The young man seated on the visitor's side of the desk had frustration etched into every line of his tanned face.

She looked up from her soiled skirt, sparks turning her hazel eyes to a flashing emerald. Taking some change from a dish in her top drawer, she ignored him and crossed the room to the cigarette machine, where she pushed the coins into the slot with a vengeance. Picking up the green and white pack of menthol cigarettes, she returned to her chair and pulled the cellophane off the pack, then extracted a long cigarette, which she placed between tight lips.

Striking the match with an angry gesture, Noel lighted the cigarette and took a long, deep breath. She refused to meet the visitor's exasperated expression as she exhaled a slim trail of wispy blue smoke toward the ceiling. Returning her attention to her skirt, her left hand continued to dab at the stain, while her right hand, trembling slightly with barely suppressed fury, moved the cigarette unsteadily to her full-cut lips.

"It's not necessary for you to continue." She finally broke the heavy silence. "You've already said more than enough, Jeff. I unequivocally refuse to interview Ross McCormick on the *Wake Up Las Vegas* program. I don't believe a football quarterback is my type of guest, and I've no intention of spending *my* time on *my* show attempting to carry on a conversation with any man whose neck size is a larger number than his IQ!"

"But, Noel—"

"No, Jeff. No but's about it. You can just trundle off and tell whatever idiot booked the man on the show to just unbook him! We've nothing further to discuss." She exhaled a furious puff of smoke, indicating the matter was closed.

"Just one more thing . . ." The young man's voice remained deceptively calm, despite Noel's atypical, scathing attack. "I neglected to mention that McCormick was booked from upstairs." He lifted his gaze heavenward. "By none other than the man himself— Ramsey Scott."

There was a significant little silence as Noel stopped sponging at the coffee stain long enough to look up at him, her hazel eyes narrowing with suspicion, although the gold flecks of anger still sparked. Ramsey

Scott's office might not quite be heaven, but the laws issued from the plush ninth-floor executive suite were certainly considered by all to be carved in stone.

"Ramsey? It was his idea? I don't believe it. Where would a man like Ramsey meet someone like Ross McCormick?"

"Simple. He's a friend of Jason Merrill's. Need I say more?" The last was uttered with an unmistakable note of triumph.

Noel sighed deeply, throwing the sodden tissue into her wastepaper basket. Drawing on the white filter tip of the cigarette, she considered the matter thoughtfully. No—no more was necessary. Ramsey Scott owned KSUN television, plus a number of radio stations and newspapers. A successful, vibrant man just entering his fifties, he counted among his friends some of the most influential people in the country. The fact that he could be acquainted with Jason Merrill, the millionaire credited with bringing a professional team to Las Vegas, was not surprising. And the fact that Jason Merrill would be seeking media exposure for his star quarterback was also not surprising.

What did surprise Noel, however, was the fact that Ramsey would suggest putting him on her program, knowing her personal history.

"I'd think, if no one else, that Jerry Kush would be a better choice to interview him," she argued feebly, naming the station's sports director.

Jeff Morrison rose from his chair, pushing an errant lock of blond hair from his brow. "I wouldn't know, Noel. I'm only a lowly editorial assistant who does what I'm told to do around here. And"—he looked pointedly at her—"I was informed, in no uncertain terms, that McCormick is slated for Monday morning's show."

He ignored her look of silent protest as he scraped

his chair away from the desk and rose to leave. "So," he tacked on dryly, "if I were you, I'd see if I could dig up a Lobos cheerleader's outfit before Monday. That seems to be the role Ramsey's cast you in." He grinned wickedly. "Aren't you glad you've got such good legs? I can't wait to see you in one of those short, perky little skirts."

He seemed to be enjoying her discomfort as he sauntered away, winking exaggeratedly at a young newswriter who'd been watching the exchange with interest. In fact, Noel noticed belatedly, the entire newsroom had witnessed the scene. Her cheeks flushed with anger as she faced their blatant curiosity head on, her flashing eyes daring one person to utter a word. Grinding out the cigarette into an enameled ashtray on her desk, she picked up the telephone and punched out a single digit.

"Hi, Kim," she began, injecting into her voice a note of cheeriness she certainly didn't feel. "Is Ramsey in?"

Noel met the attentive gaze of the man at the next desk with an icy glare, satisfied when he dropped his eyes and returned to work. As she waited for Ramsey's secretary to answer, she noted with a slight sigh of relief that the large room had returned to normal, the hum of conversation and typing filling the air.

"Noel," the voice answered in her ear, "he's out of town today. But he left a message for you." If the secretary suspected an impending confrontation, she gave no indication of it in her welcoming tone. Perhaps she didn't know of the custom of slaying the bearer of bad tidings. But, in this case, Jeff would have been the first victim, and he had looked healthy and annoyingly cocky as he'd left the newsroom.

"What's the message, Kim?"

"He wanted to remind you of the Big Brothers' fund-raising auction you agreed to attend with him this evening. He says he'll probably be too late to pick you up. You're to go ahead and meet him there, if that's all right."

Noel realized instantly that the shock of Ross McCormick had completely stricken the party from her mind. It was sponsored by a nonprofit organization that helped young, fatherless boys, and she'd been more than willing to make an appearance. In fact, she'd even donated a signed painting of hers for a celebrity auction. Noel relaxed from the stresses of her busy life by painting, and although she knew she'd never be able to earn a living at her hobby, it was nice to know it could generate some funds for a worthwhile cause. No, as angry as she was at Ramsey right then, she couldn't let him down on this.

"Is that the only word he left?" She was surprised that he hadn't predicted her reaction to Jeff's loaded bombshell and left an explanation.

"No. That's all."

"Kim," Noel began hesitantly, her mind shifting gears as she attempted to work out a solution to her latest problem, "is there any way you can get in touch with Ramsey?"

"Sorry, Noel. He told me he'd be on the run all day. You'll probably talk to him before I do—if you're going to see him tonight." The soft voice was noncommittal, and Noel was at a loss to determine just how much his personal secretary knew about all this. It was unlike Ramsey Scott to be out of touch with the office.

"Okay. And thanks," Noel said, hanging up, her smooth brow furrowed in thoughtful, distressed lines. Oh well, she had no more time to think about Ross McCormick right now.

She hurried to her dressing room and changed into

a light blue shirtwaist dress, ran a quick brush through her hair and arrived on the set moments before her program began taping. Her guest that morning was more controversial, yet much easier on her nerves than the thought of the professional quarterback. She smiled as she settled herself into the chocolate-brown chair, greeting the pretty, poised secretary who was in the process of suing a local bank for its refusal to allow her to breast-feed her baby on her coffee breaks.

The party was being held in the private home of a local horse breeder known in the extravagant circles of horse ownership for having some of the finest show Arabians in the world. He'd been Noel's guest on the program some months before and she'd learned that, to those who'd fallen under the spell of the elegant pampered animals, ownership was a labor of love— and money. Lots of it. While to most people a horse is a horse, Noel had been amazed to learn that a top Arabian stallion may be syndicated for more than a million dollars.

With this knowledge, she wasn't the slightest bit surprised to see the rooms filled with important, famous individuals. The sparkle of diamonds glittering on the women rivaled the jewellike stars studding the deep velvet canopy of the vast desert sky. Although Noel didn't have the funds to bedeck herself as many of the women present, she possessed a certain sense of style and a tall, slender grace that enabled her to hold her own in any crowd.

She'd chosen an ivory silk crepe-de-chine pants outfit with golden piping at the bateau neckline and cuffs, and tied with a wide, shiny wraparound belt of gold-toned leather. With high, gold heels, the outfit emphasized her slim frame.

Her mass of dark chestnut hair had been smoothed and tamed into a roll at her neck, feathery tendrils coaxed over her forehead, framing wide, intelligent hazel eyes. A touch of gold shadow brought out the gold flecks in her eyes, illuminating them brightly.

She didn't see Ramsey, but Noel had lived and worked in Las Vegas for enough years to know most of the people present, so she mingled easily, enjoying the party conversation. She soon found herself embroiled in a friendly but lively conversation with an Arizona congressman over water rights for their individual states.

"You have to admit, Noel, there's only so much water in the Colorado River. If Arizona doesn't receive federal funding for the Central Arizona Project, everyone may as well pack up and move back east, because the state will just dry up and blow away!"

Her attention wandered momentarily from the argument as she felt, rather than saw, someone observing her from across the crowded room. Lifting her gaze slightly beyond the congressman, her eyes locked for a suspended moment with the onlooker's. The man's dark brown eyes had a glint of interest as they viewed her across the intervening space, and a lazy grin turned up the corners of his mouth as he lifted his champagne glass to her in a silent toast. Before she could return the smile, the congressman asked an impatient question, snapping her attention abruptly back to the conversation.

"I'm sorry, Congressman Walters, what were you—"

"Noel! There you are!"

Noel breathed a sigh of relief as Ramsey's booming voice approached them, forestalling a need to reply to the congressman's question. Before responding to

Ramsey's presence, she looked up again for the stranger. The man with the dark eyes that had drawled such an appealing message.

Fanciful! That's what you're being! She scolded herself inwardly when she was disappointed to find him gone. She usually did not attribute such quixotic thoughts to such brief encounters. But her emotions had been careening along at a high pitch that day. Ever since Jeff Morrison's early-morning ambush.

Murmuring an apology, she turned toward Ramsey, who was making his way across the floor, another man in tow. To her relief, the politician melted into the crowd, no doubt buttonholing someone else on Arizona's need to receive more of the Colorado River's already-scant flow. Not too popular a topic in Las Vegas, considering the arid landscape of the state.

"Noel, I want you to meet a very dear friend of mine." Ramsey put his arm about Noel's waist and drew her nearer. "Jason Merrill. Jason, this is the young woman I've been telling you all about."

The second man shook Noel's hand, his bright eyes alight with interest. "I can see why you were raving about her, Ram. She's even more delightful than my television screen has attested to. How do you do, my dear?"

As she shook hands, Noel had to stifle a giggle. If anyone had ever asked her to venture a guess as to the appearance of Jason Merrill, she would have described someone like Ramsey Scott, perhaps a little older. Tall, with distinguished silvery hair, an imposing build, year-round tan. Someone who both looked and acted like a power broker. This diminutive man reminded her of the elfish Puck. She wondered idly how many adversaries had been caught off guard by his innocuous appearance.

"Hello, Mr. Merrill. I'm pleased to meet you." Noel smiled attractively, ignoring Ramsey's mischievous grin. He was putting her on the spot. There was no way to protest Ross McCormick's appearing on her program with Jason Merrill standing there between them!

"I'm pleased as punch to meet you, Noel. And I'm so excited about Monday morning! You know"—he leaned toward her conspiratorially—"my accountants tell me this football team should turn out to be a good business investment. But to me, it's just plain fun! I don't know when I've had a more delightful time. And Ross makes the entire enterprise even more exciting."

He looked past her for a brief moment, his attention distracted by something. "There he is now." Jason waved his arm at a point somewhere beyond Noel's left shoulder. "Ross, my boy! Come and meet some friends of mine."

"I thought you'd never ask."

Noel heard him before she turned to view him, the low, resonant voice close to her ear as he came up behind her. Turning, she was surprised to view the man who'd smiled at her earlier.

"Ross, I want you to meet Ramsey Scott and his lovely friend, Noel Heywood. Noel, Ram—meet Ross McCormick, the greatest quarterback ever to pass a football!"

"Jason exaggerates."

Ross took Noel's hand in his, allowing it to disappear for what seemed like an eternity as his smiling dark eyes made a leisurely tour of her body. The smooth chocolate gaze took in every plane of her face and engaged her hazel eyes in an unnerving sensual duel before moving down her slender frame. Unrelenting, those warm eyes embraced the soft curves molding the silk suit with the disquieting impact of a physical caress as they moved down her long, trouser-clad legs and back up again, agonizingly slowly, to her eyes.

A smile creased his tanned face, which was home to a full, fiery red beard. "Miss Heywood, this is quite a pleasure." Although his words were entirely proper, the husky, mellow tones suggested an intimacy that Noel found intensely disturbing, but not surprising. Ross McCormick was no different from any other professional athlete. The man blissfully went through life believing he was God's gift to the female population. A conviction undoubtedly substantiated by a plethora of all-too-willing women.

"Mr. McCormick," she replied curtly, her eyes hardening to brittle glass.

His face darkened perceptively with a puzzled frown. "The name's Ross," he amended, before reluctantly turning his attention to Ramsey.

"Mr. Scott."

"Call me Ram," the older man insisted, his broad white teeth flashing in a smile that was enthusiastically boyish, as if Ross McCormick were the high point of his evening. "I want you to know I've been following your career since your college days at Nebraska, and I wouldn't argue with a single word Jason has to say about you. You've brought a lot to the game, Ross. What you've done for the passing game has been nothing short of miraculous! And all us Monday-morning quarterbacks are grateful!"

Noel watched as the full-lipped sensual mouth above the blazing beard curved into an appreciative smile.

"I wish all the fans were as knowledgeable as you," he stated, his voice breaking into a deep, rich laugh.

Noel wondered at the strange effect the sound had on her nerve endings, which seemed to leap a little in response.

The three men launched into a long discussion of the game, seemingly forgetting Noel's presence, and she was free to watch Ross McCormick surreptitiously. She was forced to admit, somewhere in her most secret self, that here—like this—with the enthusiasm for the game lighting his face, Ross was a very attractive man. Breathtaking, in fact.

She knew from hard-learned experience, however, that an athlete riding the wave of popularity could be a most charming creature. Charming and lethal, like a tawny jungle cat. She recalled the limerick she'd jumped rope to so many years before in a California schoolyard—about the woman who was foolhardy enough to think she could ride on the back of a beautiful tiger:

> They came back from the ride
> With the lady inside
> And a smile on the face of the tiger.

Well, she'd been like that foolish woman once in her life. There was no way she'd ever fall into the same trap again!

At one point in the conversation, Ross's eyes slid over to her, a preoccupied look in their brown depths, then turned away. Finally, Ramsey turned to Noel as if he were surprised to find her still there.

"Noel, darling," he apologized, "how could we ramble on so and forget you like that? I am sorry."

She smiled forgiveness as Jason seconded Ramsey's apology. The icy look she turned toward Ross may have stopped any repentance from that quarter.

His face remained as bland as a slice of white bread and she noted he pointedly refrained from adding his own regrets to the murmured chorus.

Noel could definitely see why women found him so attractive. The frilled shirt and dinner jacket strained across the powerful muscles of his chest, while the cut of the black dress slacks did nothing to hide the solid strength of his thighs. The man oozed self-confidence and a sexual, animal magnetism, and she felt a shudder of apprehension as she was caught in the depths of those deep-set dark eyes.

He was too rudely male, almost pagan in his masculinity, and Noel was quite honestly more frightened of interviewing him now than she'd been that morning. She was turning away, seeking a waiter in order to get a fortifying drink, when Ramsey took her arm.

"Noel, why don't you and Ross dance while Jason and I argue a little business? There's nothing like seeing a vibrant young couple to make a man realize his own advancing years."

Ramsey's cultivated, self-assured tones were those of a man who, although he hadn't managed to halt time from passing, had made remarkable inroads against its effects. She knew he considered himself far from over the hill and eyed him with suspicion.

"Now, Ramsey," she demurred, a hint of steel in the soft tones, "you know I don't like to become too well acquainted with my guests before air time."

"It's only a dance, darling. Not a lifetime commitment," he advised her wryly.

Noel knew she was sounding churlish, but she was willing to appear so in order to avoid being alone with Ross. But it was too late. Ross was already stepping up to her. "Miss Heywood, I believe this is our dance."

Noel cast one last imploring glance at Ramsey, who

remained immovable, before shrugging her shoulders slightly in defeat.

"All right," she agreed as she stalked out onto the dance floor, Ross right behind her, "one dance."

"Are you always this gracious?" he muttered in her ear as he drew her into his arms. "Or do I just bring out your good side?"

"I'm sure you've enough women leaping at the chance to dance with the great Ross McCormick without having your heart broken on my account," she retorted caustically.

"You're right about that," he agreed smoothly. "It's just where I come from, we're taught manners. I'm always surprised when I meet someone who's so blatantly lacking in them."

Noel shot an angry glance up into his face, but he was looking over the top of her head. She was somewhat unnerved by his attitude. While she'd been dreading his expected seduction attempt, his attitude instead seemed to be one of disapproval. He confirmed her thoughts with his next words.

"Look, I don't know what your problem is, but if it makes you feel any better, I didn't exactly ask you to dance, remember? It was your boyfriend's idea."

Noel drank in a long breath of air on a gasp. "Ramsey's not my boyfriend!"

Ross looked down, the dark slant of his eyes studying her with renewed interest. "Oh? Have you told him that?"

She struggled to give her voice a dignified ring. "Not that it's any of your business," she hissed, "but it's not necessary. I've worked for Ramsey Scott for a long time. We understand each other!"

The thunderclouds that had been threatening on his tanned face disappeared, as if the sun had suddenly come out from behind a sinister dark cloud. Ross treated her to a dazzling smile as he pulled her lightly into his embrace, his hard chest pressing against the softness of her breasts under the ivory silk. The hand on her back moved down to rest upon the sensitive curve of her spine as he led her through a complicated series of steps.

"You don't know what a relief it is to discover you're a free agent," he murmured against her hair. "This is definitely turning out to be my lucky day!"

2

Noel was stunned by his infuriating confidence. She pushed against his chest, attempting to widen the space between them, but his strength was so superior she might have been trying to budge a stone wall. Ross seemed not to notice her distress; indeed, the wide hand moved even lower to mold her soft curves to his own hard length. The jolt of electricity that sparked along her nerve endings caused Noel to stumble slightly, missing a step.

Ross glanced down, giving her a quizzical look as he observed her pale face. "I think you could use a breath of fresh air," he diagnosed.

"No!" She shot out the answer, terrified at the thought of being alone with him outside. It was as if all the years of healing she'd come through had never existed. She was responding to Ross in much the same way she'd responded that first time when a college athlete had sauntered up to her, flashed some broad white teeth in a bronzed face and offered to buy her what should have been an innocuous cup of coffee. But she'd gazed upon Steve Banning with the awe of a young girl. The sensations this time were undeniably those of an adult woman.

"Look," he coaxed her somewhat wearily, "I promise I have no intention of raping you in the garden. I just think it would look a trifle odd if you were to faint right here on the dance floor. I guarantee tomorrow morning you'd wake up to read that the glamorous anchorwoman of *Wake Up Las Vegas* swooned into the arms of the Las Vegas Lobos' star quarterback at a wealthy society party. While I can always use the publicity," he grinned rakishly, "I don't think it's the image you want to portray."

"No," she repeated, shaking her head, trying to clear the swimming sensation, "I'll be fine. I just want you to take me back to Ramsey."

He danced her to the doorway and, with one firm hand on her back, literally pushed her through the open French doors into the fragrant garden.

"Not yet." He led her to a wrought-iron railing that ran along the terrace at waist height.

Noel turned away from him, gripping the railing with both hands, gulping in several deep, calming breaths of the desert night air. As usual, there was a breeze, whipping the strands of carefully coiffured hair from its imprisoned coil, the strands escaping about her cheeks in dark tendrils.

She fumbled in her gold clutch bag and pulled out a cigarette, lighting it with fingers that trembled in the moon-spangled light. The red glow of the burning tip flared for an instant as she inhaled, feeling the burning but comforting smoke filling her lungs.

"Do you do that a lot?"

Noel exhaled, eyeing him through the blue smoke.

Ross was obviously viewing her smoking with scant approval. She seemed to have a knack for irritating him, and she tried to ignore the nagging little question of just why that should bother her so.

"Not often," she answered, thinking how she'd smoked more that day than she had in the past month. After her conversation with Jeff that morning, she'd discovered it to be a satisfying, soothing habit.

"How often?"

"Just when I'm nervous." Too late, she realized she'd just handed the man some crucial ammunition.

Ross rocked back on his heels, regarding her with interest in the mellow light. "Do I make you nervous?"

"No. Parties like this do," she lied unconvincingly.

He stroked the lush red beard thoughtfully, shaking his head as he totally dismissed the idea. Noel curved her fingers tightly about her slim evening bag to keep them from reaching up to feel the beard for herself. What in the world was the matter with her?

"You'd be in your element at a party like this. If you weren't a people-type person, you'd have an entirely different occupation."

"I told you," Noel insisted quietly, "it's the party."

The lie hung heavily in the silence for a long moment, then he reached out and took the cigarette from her hand. She watched, speechless, as he dropped it to the ground and crushed it into the flagstone. Noel knew that Ross wanted to kiss her. That it had been in his mind from the first moment he'd lifted that champagne glass in his intimate, silent salute. That did not surprise her. And, if he had been anyone else, it probably would not have even upset her. As it was, she stood there, her back against the iron railing, self-consciously meeting his dark eyes, which smoldered like burning coals. The lambent flame gleaming in those brown eyes seemed to be mesmerizing her, and Noel realized that, since she'd first seen them curve into that lazy smile, she'd been wondering just how those full, sensual lips would feel.

"You have no idea," he said on a throaty, husky note as he moved nearer, lowering his head slowly, "just how long I've dreamed of this."

He was a strong man, and his voice had betrayed a surging desire, so Noel expected a harsh, demanding assault. But Ross surprised her as his lips touched hers with a silky persuasion, willing her enticingly to respond. His wide, strong hands slid caressingly over her soft curves, his fingers playing over her with a tenderness she would have thought impossible from such a large man.

His mouth was warm, gently beguiling, and her lips softened and parted to his velvet coaxing, creating an entry for his tongue. The strength drained from her as those wonderful hands slid more boldly over her body's curves, seeking forbidden intimacies; Noel felt her bones melting like heated honey.

Her hands moved up his corded arms until they were tangling in the lush, soft waves of red-gold hair at the back of his neck and she leaned her body into his male strength. Noel became alive under his clever hands, moving against him as her own seductive tongue moved to probe the moist corners of his mouth with an innate sensuality.

It was as if they were suspended in a vacuum of escalating golden desire, where reality ceased to exist. There was only this breathtaking pleasure of his mouth moving questingly on hers, lustily savoring sweet delights as the soft beard caressed her face with whispers of rapture. Noel could feel her own body beginning to spark with an answering flame as she basked in the heat of his own.

His hands moved down her back, propelling her into hard, intimate contact. A low moan escaped from his chest. The muffled sound seemed surprisingly jarring in the still, clear desert night and caused a thin thread of sanity to spark in her fevered brain. This was exactly what he'd expected. Instant conquest. Like an army marching into captured territory, it would never occur to Ross that the entire female population wasn't his for the taking.

Twisting abruptly loose from his arms, she turned away from the startled, blinking dark gaze. Her gleaming chestnut hair had come loose, dark strands falling across her cheeks. Her hands were shaking as she straightened her disheveled clothing. A hand came around, handing her the gold mesh purse he'd picked up from the flagstone where she'd dropped it.

"Thank you."

She reached into her purse for another cigarette to replace the one he'd ground under his foot. Just like my self-esteem, she thought angrily.

Ross watched her light the cigarette. "If you were my woman," he chided, eyeing her in the brief flare of orange flame, "I wouldn't let you smoke those things. You're going to kill yourself."

"I can't imagine ever being your woman," she answered acidly. "So I wouldn't concern yourself in the matter. Unless I die before Monday morning, it has nothing to do with you."

There was a flicker of something deep in the dark brown eyes that Noel found impossible to decode.

"I don't suppose you'd care to enlighten me as to what just happened?"

"Nothing," she returned with a short clip. In reality she was far more furious with herself than with him. But she was damned if she was going to let him know that. He could well argue that she'd invited that kiss. And enjoyed it. But she'd die before she'd admit it. Or before she let it happen again.

"Funny. I thought we'd just shared a most enjoyable kiss."

"All right, I stand corrected." Noel forced her tone into one of cool disregard. "Nothing important happened. Is that better?"

His eyes narrowed and they were glaring at each other like two preschoolers at opposite sides of the sandbox. Noel realized it was really quite silly for two adults to be behaving as they were. She inhaled deeply on the icy menthol, gazing out over the landscaped gardens and attempting to come up with some words that would put the entire misadventure into a better light. But, when she looked up again, Ross McCormick was gone.

"I keep losing you!" Ramsey's deep voice echoed across the terrace as he came up to Noel with long, confident strides. "If I didn't know better, I'd think you were hiding from me."

"I'd say it was more the other way around," she observed dryly. "Where were you all day?"

His gray eyes were studiously bland. "Busy. Why? Did you have a problem?" He leaned his hips back against the railing as he faced her, arms crossed against the silk-clad chest.

Distress mirrored in her hazel eyes, which shadowed slightly as she held his gray gaze and forced him to look at her directly, instead of with the obtuse, impersonal expression that he'd slid down like a mask over his features.

"A problem? Ramsey, you of all people shouldn't have to ask that. How could you schedule Ross McCormick on my program? And then go ahead and announce it to Jason Merrill so I have no alternative?"

Ramsey drew a long breath and exhaled slowly, looking past her to the flashing gaudy lights of Las Vegas's glittering strip. From her vantage point above the city, the lights were twinkling like multicolored stars in the cool night sky.

"I thought we'd agreed when you took this job that you were a professional," he stated finally. "And that I was not offering it to you in friendship, but because you were the best person for the position."

"I think I've done justice to that decision," Noel argued softly, but firmly.

"I think you have, too, Noel." His eyes returned to her, softening with affection. "And, I know you'll do a professional job Monday morning."

She opened her purse for still another cigarette. The third of the evening, she counted grimly, knowing she was going to have a killer of a headache in the morning.

"I thought you were going to quit," he observed, flicking his slim gold lighter open and shut with a precise snap.

"I did," she muttered, inhaling deeply. That was mostly true. She actually smoked very little these days. Just during times of extreme tension. It was a barometer those who knew her well had learned to read.

"Ramsey"—she struggled to keep her voice steady—"*Wake Up Las Vegas* is not the best spot for Ross McCormick. It's a light news show—with a sixty-five-percent female audience. They aren't interested in football."

"I'm betting they'll be interested in McCormick," he quipped. "Noel," he continued, spacing his words with deliberation, "professional sports bring in a lot of big-dollar revenues. Not only in gate receipts and tourism, but it's quite often a deciding factor when major companies are seeking to relocate. A professional football team in a city is a decided plus."

"I can appreciate that, but—"

"Noel," Ramsey warned sternly, "don't interrupt. I was only seeking an expanded audience. We've already got Ross slated to appear on Kush's *Sports Roundup*. I just wanted to cover all the bases."

"That's baseball."

Despite the fleeting spark of earlier irritation, Ramsey now appeared totally unperturbed as he answered. "See, you're perfect for the job. Besides being talented and beautiful, you know your sports."

He looked extremely self-satisfied as he leaned back against the railing, grinning, Noel thought, like a Cheshire cat. She shook her head in exasperation.

"Don't con me, Ramsey Scott," she threatened. "You know I should know my sports after being married to the biggest player in football for two long, miserable years!"

"That was a long time ago," he reminded her. "I think it's time to put it away."

"It was only five years ago, which is not that long. And, for your information, I had it put away until today when you threw Ross McCormick into my lap."

"I didn't throw him into your lap, darling. I only slated him for ten minutes on your program. Although I'd think you should be thanking me instead of trying to tear me to ribbons. He's quite attractive, you'll have to admit."

Noel's hazel eyes narrowed as she studied Ramsey's handsome, impassive features, wondering just how long he'd been out there before greeting her. Had he seen the display she and Ross had put on? She shrugged mentally. If there was one person from whom she had no secrets, it was Ramsey Scott.

"I've heard Bluebeard was a knockout, too," she

returned with dry sarcasm. "It's a good thing we weren't doing *Wake Up Las Vegas* back then. You'd have probably made me interview him!"

The intelligent eyes slivered as they observed her with a glint of amusement. "If he was good for the ratings," he agreed cheerfully. "Then, we're agreed? You'll interview McCormick Monday morning?"

The comment was more a statement than a question and Noel knew she would do herself no earthly good arguing further.

"I'll do it," she agreed. "But I'll hate every last minute!"

"That's what I like to hear. I'm glad we were able to settle this little matter without bloodshed."

Ramsey rubbed his hands together as if delighted, yet Noel knew there had never been any other possible outcome. Studying his full, wavy silver hair and still-trim figure, she had to admit he was quite an attractive bulldozer. When he put his mind to it, Ramsey could charm the birds right out of the silvery palo verde trees. And, she couldn't deny he'd been a very good friend. At a time when she'd needed someone very badly, Ramsey had appeared from out of the blue and taken her shattered life and helped her put it back together again.

She would never be exactly the same. Not after Steve Banning. Not all the king's horses and all the king's men could have put Noel Heywood back together again. But, Ramsey'd done the best job humanly possible, and for that she'd always be grateful.

Noel smiled, generous in her defeat. "You old fraud! You always knew you'd get your way. You've got an absolutely irresistible line."

His deep chuckle rumbled back. "Is that all I've got?"

Noel was beginning to relax, the cloud of tension created by her encounter with Ross McCormick dissipating as she fell into her usual jesting manner with Ramsey.

"No," she decided, tilting her head and allowing herself a long, studied examination. "You're handsome, sexy, and best of all—" A sudden spark of mischief lighted her eyes. "You're filthy rich. A combination no sane woman could ever resist." Her laugh bubbled merrily with the last statement.

"Could you?" he asked, his voice casual. "Could the undeniably sane and remarkably lovely Noel Heywood resist me?"

Her startled glance flew to his eyes, her cheeks going a little pink at the implication. Her relationship with Ramsey had always been so easy, even when she'd first arrived in Las Vegas, still licking her sore and tender wounds. For him to complicate matters now, by getting serious, could lead only to disaster. With both of them losing out on a valuable friendship.

"Hey"—his voice returned on a softer key—"don't look so frightened. You should know by now I was only teasing."

She continued to search his face in the moon-spangled darkness, seeking confirmation of his words.

"Noel, you know that without a doubt you are my favorite person," he replied, putting his arms about her waist. Looking down into her troubled face, his expression was genuinely affectionate. "And you also know that, given just half a chance, I could be wildly in love with you."

He put a finger over her lips to stifle her planned protest. "But, I also realize you're a very special woman. One who deserves a marriage that lasts longer than the book check-out period at the library. I've failed at three marriages and I'm not about to try again. You've done nothing so bad that you'd ever deserve me," he grinned self-deprecatingly. "So, we'll remain the best of friends, and I promise to do nothing to frighten you away."

Noel laughed uncertainly as he finished his long declaration. "You couldn't frighten me away, Ramsey."

He moved her a little away from him, holding her at arm's length while he studied her distressed face intently.

"Maybe not me," he agreed, "but anyone who falls in love with you. Look how you reacted to simply interviewing Ross McCormick," he pointed out with maddening insight. "You're still running from your first husband. And, I'd wager a guess—love."

She moved from the circle of his arms and headed back toward the French doors. He'd hit too close to home with that one. All day she'd been attempting to analyze that morning's uncharacteristic temperament. And the only valid feeling she'd been able to detect was one of fear. She was scared to death of Ross McCormick, although it had nothing to do with the man himself. It was a knee-jerk response, and Ramsey's diagnosis was too accurate for comfort.

"I don't want to talk about this morning," she stated firmly. "It had nothing to do with personal feelings. I just didn't feel a football player belonged on *Wake Up Las Vegas*."

"Sure," he answered easily, moving with her to the doors. "Whatever you say. Ready for the auction?"

Sleep eluded Noel as she tossed and turned, images of Ross McCormick continuing to whirl through her mind. Threatening, deadly, but so undeniably compelling. Her fear remained; everything he'd done only reinforced that emotion. But he'd also touched on something else during that brief, private time in the garden. He'd managed to awaken a long-suppressed, slumbering passion.

While the moment had been exhilarating, she realized the man was dangerous. He would have no scruples when it came to his sexual behavior, using women for his own selfish pleasure and needs, just as Steve Banning had done. A surfeit of women was one of the definite perks of professional sports. And, by some wild quirk of chemistry, she and Ross McCormick were explosively drawn to one another. That had been self-evident. But he was a pro—out of her league.

She banged her fist into the pillow, trying to force it into some shape that would permit her to relax and fall asleep. Finally, she gave up and, eyeing the tangled, wrinkled sheets with disdain, rose and slipped into a soft, fluffy robe. She went into the kitchen and put on a pan of milk, taking down a can of chocolate syrup and a mug from the shelf. It was that delightful time of year in Las Vegas when neither air conditioning nor heat was necessary, so the only sound in the room was the slight droning hum of the refrigerator and the chugging action as the automatic ice maker began to fill up another tray.

She pulled the pan off the stove just as the little milky bubbles began to break around the edges of the surface and mixed in a generous glob of the thick, dark sticky syrup. Stirring briskly, Noel moved across the room and pulled the draperies open. Slumping into an easy chair covered in a brilliant pattern of bright scarlet hibiscus blossoms, she curled her legs under her as she looked out the glass doors of the balcony and sipped her hot chocolate.

The sky had changed from the deep purple of night to a more shimmering silvery gray, indicating that just below the curve of the horizon the sun was preparing to make its appearance. She watched as the few remaining stars twinkled valiantly, as if attempting to hold their own in the brightening light of day.

Soon the pale silver glow turned to a mauve haze and Noel watched the soft, wispy cotton-candy clouds as tentative, pink fingers of light peeped above the horizon. Her hands circled the cocoa cup as there came a brilliant radiance over the half-lighted world. Then, like a lover returning as promised from a long night's absence, the sun broke over the horizon, gilding the wild, dappled clouds with shafts of purest gold, splintering the sky with colors of pink, crimson and orange. It rose in the sky, a majestic validation of faith, and as she watched, it sent its warming rays in wide yellow bars across her living room.

Morning had broken and Noel could avoid it no longer. Today her attention would be focused on Ross McCormick.

She put on a pot of coffee, hoping the caffeine would prove a stimulant, making up for the hours of lost sleep. While the water was dripping through the electric coffee maker, she took a long shower, leaving the water just cool enough to sting her nerve endings and rouse her from her dreary fears.

It was a job, that was all. No different from any other. And the fact that she'd felt so vulnerable the night before was only because she'd thought about the man all day. She'd allowed her imagination to create demons and horrors which weren't even there. She'd get back on a business track and everything would be fine. Because if there was one thing Noel Heywood knew she could do very well, it was her job. And she wasn't about to let Ross McCormick alter that!

She blew her hair dry, allowing it to curl naturally

about her shoulders in a soft, casual style. Dressing quickly in a pair of white corduroy jeans and a red-striped T-shirt, she forced herself to take time for a cup of coffee and a single piece of unbuttered toast. Then she left the apartment, using the garage elevator at the end of the hallway to take her to where her powder-blue Mustang was parked in its proper slot.

At the library Noel located herself in a seldom-used corner of the reference room. She waited at a long table, doodling absently on a large yellow legal pad while the librarian gathered up the materials she'd requested.

"Here you are, Miss Heywood. Fifteen years. We don't go back any further," she apologized, pushing a cart loaded with back issues of sports magazines and microfiche copies of the issues that had been converted to the more convenient storage system.

"This will be fine. My goodness, there are quite a few, aren't there?" Noel looked at the stacks with dismay.

"I pulled only the months you requested. You *did* ask for them."

There was a hint of censure in the voice and Noel became immediately apologetic. Some librarians seemed to treat their duties as sacred missions—educating the barbarians, so to speak—and their libraries as holy mosques. Noel seemed to have latched onto a zealot.

"You're absolutely right. I did. And you don't know how much I appreciate your help. I don't know how I could do my work without you people," she added truthfully.

The elderly woman lifted her glasses from an ample bosom to the bridge of her nose, peering at Noel as if she suspected her of some veiled sarcasm. But Noel smiled her sweetest smile and the woman turned away with a muffled, "Humph!"

"For heaven's sake," Noel scolded herself under her breath, "you're only looking for a little background information on the guy—not seeking the Holy Grail!"

She gazed hesitantly at the stacks of dog-eared magazines, wondering just where to begin the seemingly herculean task she'd assigned herself.

3

Digging in, Noel wasn't surprised to find Ross McCormick featured in quite a number of the magazines. She attempted to keep her mind on her work, jotting down various statistics she found useful, but her recalcitrant mind refused her instructions to stick to work.

Instead, it brought swirling up before her Ross McCormick's smooth, melted-chocolate gaze, that soft admiring glance she'd first witnessed when he saluted her from across the room. And even now she was experiencing that quiver of pleasure that had skimmed up her spine as he'd held her close, his strong hands fingering the delicate bones of her back while his chin rested on the top of her head, his warm breath fanning her hair.

There was a very logical reason for her response, Noel assured herself. After all, he'd been the first man to hold her in his arms and kiss her with any degree of passion for a very long time. Her relationship with Ramsey had been so safe it had taken on the comfort of an old shoe. The relationship, which in the beginning had been a godsend, had become a self-imposed prison where she'd locked herself away from involvement with men. Ramsey and work. That's what had filled her life after she'd escaped from her disastrous marriage. And it was all she needed. All she wanted.

At that moment, as if on cue, Noel flipped the page, and there gazing out from its slick, colored pages was a photograph of Steve Banning. It was the year he'd won the Heisman Trophy at Stanford. Before his failure as a starting quarterback for the Wisconsin Lumberjacks. And before he turned his scoring drives from the gridiron to other women.

"Never again," she vowed in a harsh whisper, slamming the magazine shut. She had her life in full gear now, having licked her wounds and climbed to the top of her field in a town that would never know that Noel Heywood, for two miserable years, had been Noel Banning, wife of one of the NFL's annual recruiting disappointments.

For the first time in more than five years, the next day Noel tuned in her radio to a Sunday-afternoon football game. Assuring herself it was only in the line of duty, she followed every play as the Las Vegas Lobos defeated the Rams, 28–21. She grudgingly admitted Ross certainly lived up to his reputation as he captained an almost-flawless game. But, she reminded herself ruthlessly, like all professional athletes, he was just as aggressive off the playing field. She wished she'd never heard of the man!

If you really think that, pestered a little voice in the far pockets of her mind, then why are you so worried about how you'll look tomorrow?

She glanced disparagingly about her bedroom, taking in the scattered clothing that had been flung onto chairs and the bed after being tried on and discarded.

I always care how I look on television, she argued to herself, striving to believe every word. It's important to the image of the station. Noel attempted to ignore the nagging question as she tried on still another outfit.

Monday morning she was up, as usual, before the sun. *Wake Up Las Vegas* was seen live at seven A.M., which necessitated her early arrival at the station. Although her working hours were not conducive to an exciting nightlife, she was content. That is, she had been. Until now.

This morning she was undeniably edgy, apprehension wrapping its icy fingers about her heart. She always experienced a tiny flutter of butterflies in her stomach before a program, but it had never disturbed her before. She felt it kept her on her toes, not permitting her to become too casual about the effort she put out five mornings a week. But this was entirely different. Today she was a wreck! She vowed not to allow herself to set eyes on Ross McCormick until the moment he appeared on the set, and afterward to escape as soon as possible. That way, she wouldn't be forced to talk to him on a personal level.

She was blow drying her dark hair and drinking her wake-up cup of coffee when the doorbell chimed. Not believing her eyes, she stood in the open doorway facing the object of all her anguish, the cup almost dropping from her hand.

Ross took it from her, then gave her a crooked grin. "Aren't you going to invite me in?"

"Why?" Noel asked ingraciously.

He leaned one broad shoulder against the doorjamb, looking down at her from his lofty height with amused regard. "Because I'm your guest today."

She moved to shut the door on him. "At the studio," she responded through gritted teeth, *"not* my apartment!"

He deftly slid his shoulder between the door and the frame he'd been lounging against, pushing the door back open with ease. "We need to discuss that."

Giving up on her ability to keep him out, Noel turned her back and strode angrily across the room, reeling to glare at him.

"Anything we need to discuss, Mr. McCormick, we can discuss later. On the program. At the studio," she tacked on pointedly.

Ross held the cup out toward her. "Do you have any more of this? I could really use a cup of coffee."

Noel looked up at him, her hazel eyes widening with astonishment. She might as well have been talking to a brick wall. Had the man simply been hit in the head too many times?

"Didn't you hear me?" she asked.

He seemed completely at ease, ignoring her rising fury. "I heard you." He moved across the room with a lazy, athletic grace, past her into the kitchen. "Is this where you're hiding the coffee?"

"I could call the manager and have you thrown out!"

Noel followed him into the tiny kitchen area, which was only a small island in her apartment, and was disturbed to discover he practically filled the narrow area. She was left no choice but to stand uncomfortably close to him.

"You could," he agreed with maddening cheerfulness, opening cupboards until he found the one he was looking for. Taking down a heavy mug, he poured a cup of coffee from the carafe of her electric drip coffee maker and cupped the steaming mug with long, graceful fingers.

"But," he continued, looking at her with a devilish gleam in his dark brown eyes, "there you'd be—inviting scandal again." His full-carved lips tilted into a broad teasing grin. "How do you manage to keep yourself out of the news? You're much too impetuous for your own good."

"I'm not impetuous at all!"

Ross gazed down at her over the top of the mug, his eyes reminding her of the other evening, daring her to deny her reckless response. "Oh no?" he asked with a tantalizing drawl. "Do you always kiss men like that when you first meet them?"

Noel flushed an angry, humiliated crimson. He was an absolutely hateful, insufferable man and she wished he'd never entered her life, let alone her apartment! She turned away, gripping at the edge of the counter top.

He didn't even have to move in the small enclosure. He just reached out and put his hands lightly on her shoulders, turning her gently toward him.

"I'm sorry. I was just teasing." His warm, cocoa-colored eyes echoed the seemingly sincere statement. "I came by because I thought we'd better reach some kind of understanding before we appear on the air together. Unless," he said grinning, inviting her to share in the humor, "your audience is into coed wrestling with their cornflakes. Do you prefer mud or mats?"

Noel raised her wary gaze to his, relieved to find only the flickering easy humor. "All right," she agreed tentatively. "I'll stop if you will."

"Agreed!" His hands were lightly massaging her shoulders, his baritone voice deep and provocative. "Want to kiss and make up?"

She jerked away, pulling her cherry-pink robe tightly about her body. "Certainly not. And you're cheating already!"

Ross shrugged that lazy insolence that caused an angry flame to rise in her chest once again. He studied her with a long, measured appraisal, taking in her shawl-collared, wrapped robe of soft, plush pile. The rolled neckline was open slightly, the skin at the base of her neck splashed with beads of water from her recent shower.

"Then," he suggested, "you'd better get dressed. Not only do we have to be at the studio soon, you could get in a lot of trouble entertaining men before the sun comes up wearing nothing but a smile and that delightful pink confection." He stroked his coppery beard as he had Friday night, the action slow and deliberate. "Not that I've seen the smile yet."

At his assertion Noel's cheek brightened to equal the hue of the cherry-colored robe. His brown eyes lighted with success as he realized his shot in the dark had just scored a bull's-eye. While only guessing, her reaction had confirmed there was only the lush, soft material between her flesh and him. Knowing what he was thinking caused an involuntary shiver to pass over her. Ross's expression, however, remained infuriatingly bland as he sipped on the steaming, fragrant coffee.

Noel left her bedroom door ajar, keeping a cautious eye on him as she finished drying her hair and putting on her makeup. He seemed totally at ease as he moved about her living room, stopping to pick up various small items from time to time and examining her paintings. The most vivid of the bold, bright splashes adorning her walls were of enormous, vibrant flowers that made the observer want to reach out to touch the velvety, dewy petals. It was a freedom of expression that Noel rarely allowed to surface in her calm, collected appearance.

Ross stopped with interest before another canvas which depicted a winter scene. Subtly colored in grays, it was double-matted in white and framed in polished aluminum. It was out of place in the room of bright and happy colors and he turned toward the bedroom, his glance curious.

"Are you from back east?"

"No, California."

"This doesn't look like California."

Noel shook her head, concentrating on pinning her thick, glossy hair into the confinement of its roll. "It's not. It's a farmhouse in France."

He looked back at the painting intently, studying the beautiful but stark and cold landscape. "Have you ever been there?"

"No," she mumbled, her mouth full of hairpins. "I bought it because it reminded me of a couple winters I spent in Wisconsin."

Ross turned his head back to her, eyes narrowing slightly, causing a wrinkling of the wide forehead above auburn eyebrows.

"They must have been bleak winters," he commented finally.

She drove the final pin in harshly, gouging her scalp. "They were."

Noel could tell by his expression that Ross felt inclined to continue the conversation and she wanted no part of it. She didn't even like the man—to share the most dismal part of her life with him was unthinkable! She shut the bedroom door to get dressed.

He'd rinsed both cups and was waiting for her when she emerged from the bedroom clad in a royal-blue silk blouse and matching pants topped with an emerald-green suede vest. She knew the bold colors were exceedingly attractive with her bright coloring, but his gaze was neutral and he appeared not to notice.

"Ready?" he asked, moving toward the door.

"Yes. Is your car parked downstairs?"

"Sure is." He grinned for a moment, causing a vague fluttering response from the butterflies that had taken up permanent residence in her stomach. "It's parked in a no-parking zone. Think we've lost it?"

"A no-parking zone?"

She couldn't believe it. Did all professional athletes think the rules and laws others were expected to live by were automatically waived for them? Because they happened to be grown men who played a child's game?

"We'd better go see," she said, shaking her head in exasperation.

Directly outside the heavy glass doors of her apartment building sat a sleek black Porsche and she knew instantly it belonged to him. Placed in front of the low-slung car stood the red and white No Parking sign. If he had driven two more inches, he would have knocked it over.

"You're lucky it wasn't towed away." Noel turned on him. "Why couldn't you have parked where it was legal?"

"I didn't want you to have to walk so far this early in

the morning," he replied, flashing her a smile she knew from instinct he used regularly to thaw out women. It was a devastatingly beautiful smile and it only made her all the more determined to hate him. If the man thought he could get around her that easily—well, he had another guess coming. Noel Heywood was one woman he wouldn't find listed in his seduction playbook.

"I wouldn't have been here at all," she answered with an overt strain of annoyance in her voice. "My car's properly parked in the underground garage."

"Ah, but you're coming with me."

She shot him an astonished look. "I am not!"

Ross opened the door on the sidewalk side, gesturing her into the lush interior. "Of course you are. I drove all the way over here. Doesn't it seem a little foolish for both of us to leave, headed in the same direction, in separate cars?"

"No one invited you," she reminded him acidly.

"You did," he replied, leaning his arms on the top of the opened door.

"I did not."

He pushed up a sleeve on his V-necked, biscuit-colored cashmere sweater and glanced at the wide scuba-diver's watch on his wrist. "If we don't get started," he warned, "we'll be late."

Expelling a long, aggravated sigh, Noel gave up arguing and flung herself into the contoured bucket seat.

"I did not," she muttered, after he'd come around and slid his long length into the driver's seat.

His rugged cheek creased attractively above the flaming beard as he looked over at her before turning the key in the ignition. "Of course you did," he repeated with exaggerated patience. "When you kissed me like that Friday night."

Noel refused to answer the soft taunt, keeping her head straight ahead as she looked stonily out the front window. Still, she couldn't help being vibrantly aware of his strength as he shifted the car through the gears. She watched surreptitiously from beneath lowered lashes as his firm legs, clad in dark brown slacks, flexed and relaxed beside her, working the clutch of the powerful car.

"You know," he commented after a long silence, "if you knew anything about football, you'd know better than to interview a player the Monday morning after a game. You're lucky I can move to drag my aching bones to your studio." His eyes lighted up with a sudden glint. "I should have made you come interview me in the whirlpool. Sounds like more fun anyway, doesn't it?"

Her attention had been riveted on his leg and her eyes flew guiltily to his face, being met with an amused glance. He'd caught her appraisal and was loving every minute of it.

"I should think you'd be able to move all right," she managed to answer briskly. "You were only sacked once yesterday."

A wild red brow lifted questioningly. "Oh, did you go to the game?"

"No. I don't go to football games." It was expelled with such bitterness that he turned his head toward her again in interested speculation.

"Then how did you know I was sacked?"

"I listened to the game on the radio," Noel admitted. "Part of the game. Just a few minutes." She added the last dismissingly, as if to deny she'd experienced a moment's interest.

Ross returned his attention to the road. His eyes were unreadable as she watched the slight tracery of fanlike lines around them.

"I'm glad you listened."

"Only because it's my job," she inserted quickly. "I felt I should at least try to catch a few minutes of your game before interviewing you."

"Makes sense," he agreed pleasantly.

4

Noel certainly hadn't planned for things to go so horribly, but later, looking back, she knew the interview was doomed the instant she'd walked into the studio with him. There was more staff on hand than usual for the hour of the morning, and to an individual, they all seemed to be awaiting the arrival of Ross McCormick.

Every woman, from the receptionist to the new camerawoman, was suddenly alert and fawning all over him. The sight brought back all those degrading scenes she'd been forced to witness week after week outside the Lumberjacks' locker room. Her stomach lurched betrayingly, the butterflies becoming giant condors. Even the men, she noted, were hovering about, clutching little bits of paper they hoped he'd endorse.

When she saw Timothy Martin, the sound engineer,

request an autograph "for my six-year-old son," she shook her head in disbelief. Tim wasn't even married! What *was* it about these men who played games for a living that made others lift them to such exalted status?

To Ross's credit, Noel acknowledged reluctantly, he was taking it all in stride, smiling on cue and appearing not to mind the various items being thrust forward for his signature. Neither did he seem to be taking it all that seriously.

The comfortable studio set had never seemed so small and cramped before, as Ross appeared to loom larger than life over her. He had a latent energy that emitted waves of electricity crackling about her, and Noel responded like an arch-backed cat before a thunderstorm. She didn't realize she'd let her emotions get the better of her until they broke for a commercial and her producer's grating voice burst in over her hidden earphone.

"For God's sake, Noel! This is an early-morning show, remember? Keep it light. You're handling it like the Spanish Inquisition. Why don't you back off and give the poor guy a chance to discuss football, and not defend his love life?"

She pressed her lips together, casting her eyes upward to the control booth. She could tell Ross knew she'd been duly chastised. His expression remained a benign, polite mask during the remainder of the sixty-second break, but his eyes glinted merrily.

Noel turned to him as the camera light flashed on again, the red light cuing her. "There's an interesting argument brewing in certain circles, Mr. McCormick," she began, her voice saccharine sweet as she gave him a bright, false smile. "Perhaps you, as an expert, can clear it up for us?"

A trace of suspicion at her abrupt about-face mirrored in his dark eyes. "I'll certainly try," he offered obligingly.

She still smiled, her mind whirling with anticipatory glee as she continued, drawing him into her neat little trap.

"There are those who would suggest that a fan can only find the exciting, breakaway run that means so much to your game in collegiate football. They insist the professionals don't know how to run the ball. Or, indeed, they know, having received some of the best running quarterbacks in the nation from the colleges—but they simply choose to waste their talents. Would you agree with that?"

His eyes darkened slightly in surprised response to her new line of attack, but he smiled back at her, revealing nothing.

"I'd certainly agree the pros are getting great kids from the colleges," he answered. "As to the running game versus the passing game—" He lifted his shoulders in a dismissing shrug. "The object of the game is to get the ball down the field. It doesn't make a lot of sense to run—when it's easier and quicker to pass."

That was exactly what Noel had expected him to say, and her hazel eyes lighted in unconcealed pleasure as she sensed a victory right around the corner.

"If that's so," she pressed on with ingratiating politeness, "that the pass is faster—then increased passing in a game *should* mean more plays, due to incompletions and interceptions stopping the clock. Yet"—she leaned toward him, drawing the noose a bit tighter, the wicked gleam in her eye undetected by the camera but not missed for a moment by him—"it's an interesting fact that where a fan usually sees a hundred forty plays per game from the college teams, the pros can offer up an average of only a hundred thirty plays per game."

She mentally kicked the chair out from under him, leaving him to hang there, undefended. "Would you care to explain that?"

Ross leaned back in his chair, lacing those wonderful long fingers together loosely. "Well, if you're good enough not to get intercepted or have incompletions, you don't stop the clock," he answered with a deep, rolling chuckle.

Noel heard with irritation the sporadic outburst of laughter from the watching crew and audience. Persisting, she asked with barely concealed insolence, "And are *you* that good, Mr. McCormick? Not to have your passes incompleted or intercepted, I mean," she added, becoming momentarily flustered by his suggestive, devilish grin.

Ross crossed his arms over his broad chest, smiling pleasantly, but his dark brown eyes promised reprisals.

"I'd love to say I was, but no, even I get intercepted once in a while," he admitted readily. "By the way," he continued, his tone as smooth as newly churned butter, "that's quite an interesting little statistic you've dug up there. But it's not complete."

"No?" Her voice was as chilly as dry ice.

"No. The NFL runs fewer plays for several reasons: first of all the pros have a thirty-second time clock, where the college players have twenty-five seconds to put the ball into play. That's a sixteen percent difference. If the pros were to add sixteen percent to their total plays, they'd top the number. Easily. In addition, pro strategies are more complicated and they eat up more time."

Noel wasn't going to let him get off that smoothly. "Even so," she argued, stubbornly refusing to give up, "I'm sure I'm not the only fan out here who considers a running game more productive and imaginative. It's a fact that professional teams consistently fall short of two hundred yards rushing per game. A figure any good college coach would consider a bare minimum." There. Let him wiggle out of *that* one!

The muscle tensing along the growth of russet beard was the only sign of his irritation as he leaned forward, hands spread on his knees.

"That's an average. And it's also a fact that college teams manage to make those high numbers rushing against teams that spend each season operating as perpetual losers, just to earn the money to keep their athletic departments alive for another year. The four hundred yards that can be rolled up rushing on the ground in those running games more than makes up for the close ones, where they can't work their option plays. And there's another reason why the professional teams stick to the passing game. One I'm grateful for, myself."

"And that is?" Noel inquired, her tone getting more wintry brisk with each word. The temperature in the studio, even under the hot lights, would have rivaled the iciest day in Wisconsin.

Ross turned away from her to grin into the camera, inviting the audience to succumb to his infectious smile.

"A linebacker chasing a running quarterback is just about the happiest guy in football," he explained. "Running an option, you can only string it out so far. Then you have to turn upfield. And that's when the defensive man just grins with pleasure. One hit can take off the quarterback's head. And pretty soon— well, you'd find yourself flat out of quarterbacks."

Noel smiled indulgently. "Come now, wouldn't you have to admit that's a bit of an exaggeration?"

He swiveled suddenly in the brown chair, leaning his right shoulder toward her. "Touch it," he instructed tightly.

"I don't really believe this is necessary." Noel forced a weak laugh.

His eyes were jet black in a face chiseled in stone. "Touch it," he repeated softly.

"You got yourself into this, Noel, baby," the voice in her earphone instructed. "Now, you'd better go along and see if you can salvage your last three minutes."

She reached over hesitantly, running her fingers lightly over his cashmere-clad shoulder. While firm and muscled, it didn't feel as smooth as she might have suspected.

"It's partly synthetic," he answered her questioning look. "I was running an option play on short yardage. The week before, I'd been hit and dislocated my shoulder. They'd pinned it back into place. That's what you do in the pros," he informed her, as if instructing a rather dense kindergarten student. "You get yourself taped back together to go out there again. I was running that play—that option you're so fond of—when I was blind-sided. They tell me you could hear the impact up in the press box. It knocked the pin out and now I have this." He rubbed his shoulder. "Amazing what they can do with plastics these days, isn't it?"

Noel realized that the sympathies of her audience were quite properly now solely with him. He'd slipped the noose and gotten away.

"But, as dreadful as that must have been, you were only hit once yesterday," she reminded him, one last feeble try.

Ross nodded, his copper-colored hair falling lightly over his forehead. "That's because we use the passing game. The ball's out of my hands before that lineman can reach me. Last season Kevin Johnson caught eighty-six passes, the second leading pass receiver in the NFL. Our two wide receivers, Jimmy Matthews and Chuck Freeman, caught one hundred and seventy passes between them. I think we were able to please the fans with those plays."

He smiled engagingly into the unblinking camera lens, before turning back to Noel, his eyes shouting his undeniable victory.

Noel smiled back, this time sincerely, in admiration of the deft way he'd handled himself. His agility was not only physical. He'd outthought her at every turn.

"From the way this town is caught up in Lobos Fever," she agreed, "I'd say you've definitely given them their money's worth. And you've given us our money's worth today, Ross. Thanks for coming."

He inclined his head. "It was fun, Noel. Let's do it again sometime."

She stifled her look of surprise, realizing he was only saying lines appropriate to the occasion. "When you guys win the Super Bowl," she promised.

Turning back toward the number-one camera, she closed, much to the relief of every anxious person crowded into the control room.

"We've been chatting with Ross McCormick, thirteen-year pro and now the popular quarterback for our Las Vegas Lobos. This is only the second season for the expansion team, and they're rolling up winners like a rigged slot machine, to the delight of residents and visitors alike. Catch a bit of Lobos Fever at the stadium this Sunday. You'll be glad you did. This is Noel Heywood, saying for KSUN television, *Have a lucky day, Las Vegas!*"

"Now that that's over with, how about breakfast?"

Noel turned to Ross in surprise as she unpinned the microphone from the curve of her emerald vest. "Breakfast?"

"I'm starving and I know you only had coffee. Don't famous television celebrities eat?" His sparkling eyes traveled over her slim frame.

"Of course, but—"

He held up a hand. "No buts about it. And I'm going to let you put it on your expense account so you can't object to it as a date."

He proceeded to override every weak excuse Noel could think up and she soon found herself with him in a red vinyl booth at a coffee shop a few blocks away from the station.

"You know a lot about football," he commented, taking two slices of golden buttered toast from the stack in front of them and placing them on her plate, indicating with a stern expression that she was expected to eat them. "I wasn't expecting that. I thought we'd do more of a puff piece. A light look at an average day. Something like that."

Noel dropped her eyes, intent on stirring sugar into her coffee. "I'm sorry about that. I don't know what came over me."

Ross put his hand over hers on the table, causing her to look up in distress. But his eyes were warm and gentle.

"Hey, it's okay. I don't get many people willing to take me on anymore. The press always seems too busy with their mythmaking to ask any tough questions. I liked it. You can knock me off my pedestal any old day."

Her answering smile was ruefully weak. How could she have done such a thing? It was totally out of character and she knew she must have come off looking like an absolute shrew. Medusa would have been a sweetheart compared to the scene she'd just played out on live television!

"At least I should have eased up on you."

"Forget it. You actually managed to have the audience feeling sorry for me. It's been a long time since I've been an underdog. I enjoyed it."

He offered her the orange marmalade. "Where did you learn all that technical jargon? Not this weekend listening to just part of a game."

Noel shook her head to both the marmalade and the question, pushing her plate slightly away from her. She pulled a cigarette out of her purse and Ross took the slim lighter from her hand, flicking it as he observed her contemplatively over the bright orange flame.

"Am I making you nervous again?"

"A little," she admitted.

She lapsed into silence as she smoked. Seeming unwilling to pressure her, Ross returned his attention to the fried hash-browned potatoes on his plate.

"It's really no secret, I guess," she offered finally, in a small, quiet voice. "I was married to a football player. A long time ago."

His fork stopped in midair on the way to his mouth. "College or pro?" The keen brown eyes took in her slightly shaking hands as she inhaled deeply, borrowing time before answering.

"Both."

"Who?"

Noel didn't have to tell him. It would reveal too many private pains to lay out her soul—naked and unprotected—there on the scratched and nicked green Formica tabletop for him to observe. But she wasn't going to keep it from him. She decided rashly to cast caution to the four winds and trust this tall man with hair and full beard the color of burnished autumn leaves.

"Steve Banning."

It was only a name—not a life history. But it spoke volumes. Compassion touched his eyes and his features softened.

"I see. I'm sorry, Noel."

She lifted her slim shoulders in a slight shrug, fighting a losing battle to keep her full lips from trembling. "It was a long time ago."

His eyes narrowed fractionally, studying her for what seemed an immeasurable time. "I'd say not long enough," he commented finally.

She briskly changed the subject as she felt the hot, stinging tears behind her eyelids. Good grief, it had been years since she'd cried over Steve Banning! What was the matter with her? Perhaps she was coming down with something. Her thoughts had been so tumultuous the past few days, her emotions refusing to remain on the taut leash she'd confined them to so many years before.

"And what about you? What are you going to do when you finish with professional ball? None of the articles I found said what your major had been at Nebraska."

Ross stretched his long legs under the table and Noel felt a tingle of alarm race through her veins as his thigh brushed hers. Alarm and something else. What was it? Pleasure? Desire? A virus, she decided firmly. Most definitely a virus.

"I majored in communications," he answered.

Just what the world needs, another sportscaster. Why did they all think just because they could throw a ball or swing a bat they could also talk intelligently and coherently on camera? She'd worked hard to achieve the level of proficiency she'd acquired thus far. A master's in broadcasting, and all the years in Wisconsin and then here that she'd spent honing her craft, while they all seemed to believe they could shuck their uniforms, slip into a brightly colored blazer and have it made. Although, she admitted, it *was* possible this one could join the ranks of his colleagues who'd succeeded.

His deep laugh rumbled from that solidly muscled chest, causing the already interested waitress leaning against the counter to glance at him more avidly.

"You thought I was just another dumb jock, didn't you?"

Noel blushed a bright crimson, realizing he'd read her thoughts. "No," she denied lamely. "I didn't think that . . . exactly."

Ross reached over and put his fingers under her chin, lifting her face as he held her anxious hazel gaze with his own appealing one. "You did. Exactly," he mimicked.

"I was only picturing you as a sportscaster."

Brown eyes danced at her obvious discomfort. "Who said anything about sportscasting?"

"Didn't you?"

"Nope." He shook the tawny head. "It must have been when you were dreaming about me. Sometimes it's hard to keep our dreams separate from reality. You should hear about some of the starring roles you've been cast in lately." His grin was definitely suggestive and Noel turned away.

"I've gone back to school in the off-season," he offered, not causing her to probe any further. "And gotten my law degree. So you see," he said, a lazy grin turning the corners of his mouth as she looked at him in surprise, "I do have a brain on these rather deteriorating shoulders. Which is why I prefer the passing game. I'd hate to get it scrambled before I get a chance to practice."

Her voice was scarcely audible. "Oh. That's very interesting."

He smiled at her with a boyish, crooked grin. "I think so. How about you? What does Noel Heywood see herself doing five years from now?"

"Anchoring a network nightly news program," she answered promptly, the answer being an easy one. She kept the goal out there in front of her at all times. The pot of gold at the end of her video rainbow. The problem was, she'd admit to herself on days of flagging confidence, it was also the goal of practically every man and woman who ever clipped on a microphone and faced a television camera.

"Anybody else sharing this picture of success with you?" Ross inquired casually. "Husband? Kids? Cocker spaniel puppy?"

"Nary a soul. I think I've discovered I'm cut out to live by myself." She smiled, hiding her actual thoughts. "I've horrible habits no sane person would ever put up with. I go to bed before double digits on my clock radio; I'm up when most people are just beginning the good dreams. I'll take off anywhere, anytime, to get a story. Because I never know. This one may just be the big break. The one that'll shoot me up to the big time. Nobody in his right mind would live with that."

"Could get lonely," was the only comment.

"There's a vast difference between being alone and being lonely, Ross. I like living alone. It suits me."

Truthfully, it was one of the regrets of her life that she hadn't had a child. Earlier, during the disastrous years of her marriage, she'd known the armed camp under fire she shared with Steve Banning was no home into which to bring a child. She'd waited in vain for things to work out before starting a family. It was almost ironic, in a sense, that Steve's fathering another woman's child, and the resulting paternity suit, had been the final straw in their farce of a marriage.

Later, after the divorce, Noel had grown to realize that she was actually fortunate there'd been no children. It would have been extremely difficult to build her career and try to be both mother and father as well. No, she'd come to terms with her life. And, except for an occasional pang, she was quite satisfied.

The conversation dwindled off while they both finished their coffee.

When he dropped her back at the studio, Ross leaned over to open the door for her. He'd double-parked, she noted, then felt a surge of warmth as his arm brushed against her.

"What time shall I pick you up?" he asked, the engine of the Porsche humming smoothly as it idled in front of the KSUN building.

"Pick me up?"

"You need a lift home. I'm going to provide it."

Noel had forgotten about leaving her Mustang sitting in the garage. "I can call a cab, Ross."

He turned toward her, his right arm resting on the back of her seat, dangerously close. If she put her head back right now, just a little bit, she'd be able to feel its warmth. She sat up straighter, denying her rebellious body what it was crying out for so loudly.

"That's silly," he answered lightly. "It's my fault you're without transportation, so I'll pay my debt and drive you home. That way we'll have a chance to discuss where we're going this evening."

"Going?" She was sounding like a parrot, echoing everything he said. But it seemed the man was always one step ahead of her, and she was forced to be constantly struggling to keep up.

"You bought my breakfast. I intend to reciprocate by taking you out to dinner."

Noel gave a slow shake of her head. "That was business."

His rugged features creased into an attractive, coaxing smile. "I know. And tonight will be pleasure."

The dark eyes shimmered bronze with promise and she once again experienced that flame licking along her veins. There in the small car with him she could feel herself succumbing to the warm muskiness of the leather, which mingled with a distinctive scent that had assailed her senses the other evening. A scent Noel recognized to be all his own. It both disturbed and aroused her, and she realized that if she were to feel like this at nine-thirty in the morning, on a sun-brightened street, it would be suicide to allow herself another moment alone with him.

Especially at night. In an atmosphere he'd already warned her would be designed for pleasure. His pleasure or hers? Noel considered the problem briefly, before admitting to the fact that to feel those lips once more on hers, those hands caressing her body, could only be mutually rewarding.

But not satisfying. There was a great amount of sexual energy in Ross McCormick; she could feel it even now, swirling about them like a crackling summer storm. She knew the man would never be satisfied with a simple kiss. No, the thing to do was to get out of the car while escape was still possible.

Noel put her hand on the door handle. "Thanks anyway, Ross. But remember, I'm a working girl. I can't stay up late and do justice to my job."

He reached out and caught her hand, cutting off her flight. "I know that," he said simply. He kept her hand clasped in his while his other hand opened the glove compartment of the car. Pulling out a small magazine, he dropped it into her lap.

"Here. Check tomorrow's listings."

Noel looked down bleakly at the television guide. She knew what it would say. She didn't have to look. Ross's thumb made sensual circles on her imprisoned palm as he watched the play of emotions cross her face—from surprise, to dismay, to defeat.

"I warned you not to sell me short. I really do know how to read. And it states in there that tomorrow's edition of *Wake Up Las Vegas* will be canceled due to coverage of the space shuttle landing. So you see"—the deep voice was matter-of-fact, denying opposition—"you can come out tonight, Cinderella, without turning into a pumpkin, after all."

Noel gave him a wobbly smile. "I don't suppose you'd believe I forgot?"

"Nope."

"I still don't know—"

"Let's try something," Ross suggested, his voice velvety smooth, almost a physical caress. "Why don't you pretend you've got a dinner date with an attorney who thinks you're the most breathtaking woman he's ever met? All he wants from life is the chance to take this beautiful, intelligent woman out to dinner. No pressure. No strings."

His eyes were as dark, smooth and brown as fine Swiss chocolate. "And while you're pretending that, Noel, believe that if he'd ever imagined he'd meet this incredible woman who hated athletes—he never would have picked up a ball in the first place!"

5

His thumb was causing a restless fluttering deep inside her and Ross could read her awakening feelings in the wide, confused hazel eyes as she unconsciously leaned toward him. He bent to meet her, his mouth approaching her slightly parted lips, when the blare of a loud horn behind them sent them both jumping apart.

"Damn!" The word exploded from his lips.

It suddenly struck Noel as humorous, the two of them being caught like a pair of lovesick adolescents. Her laugh bubbled as she patted his strong arm.

"That's what you get for double-parking," she teased. "One of these days you'll learn to obey the laws."

She opened the door and jumped out onto the sidewalk, waving apologetically to the man waiting behind them in the pickup truck. Bending down to say good-bye before closing the door of the black sports car, Noel said, "I'll be ready about two o'clock, if that's all right with you."

A flush of pleasure replaced the startled look on his face. "I'll be here. And parked legally, too."

Noel grinned, feeling unusually lighthearted. "I'll believe that when I see it," she replied, shaking her dark head and running to disappear into the building.

The low, droning hum of conversation ceased abruptly as Noel entered the large newsroom, heads swiveling as if on magnets at her approach. She got the unmistakable impression that she'd been the subject under discussion—a feeling that was heightened when the intercom on her desk buzzed insistently.

"Noel? I heard you were back." Ramsey's secretary sounded strained.

"Kim, I think you know everything around here two minutes before it happens," Noel laughed.

"Noel, this is serious," Kim stressed. "Mr. Scott has asked to see you the second you come in."

"Tell Ramsey I'll be right up," she promised. She took out her compact to reapply her lip gloss and stopped for a moment to study her reflection. An attractive light was dancing in her eyes, causing the gold flecks to gleam warmly. Her full lips were curved in a reminiscent smile and a faint flush outlined her cheekbones, resembling the bloom of late-summer roses.

"You'll do," she decreed, murmuring to herself before closing the compact with a decisive click. Suddenly, she was in a terrific mood!

"I thought I'd instructed Kim to tell you I wanted to see you immediately." Ramsey was seated stiffly behind his desk, clad impeccably in a custom-tailored navy-blue suit.

"I came as soon as I could," she answered calmly. "What's the problem?"

An incredulous look passed over his usually controlled features. "'What's the problem?' How in the name of heaven can you even ask that? Weren't you in the studio this morning?"

She sat in a chair across from the desk, crossing her long legs comfortably in a fluid, graceful motion. "Of course I was. I did the show. The one with Ross McCormick you suggested."

"Aha! Now, it's 'suggested'! Last Friday you swore I was *forcing* you to do the program." His face darkened with an angry flush.

Noel clasped manicured fingers loosely around one knee and leaned back in the chair, her pose one of total relaxation. It was as if her time spent with Ross had dulled her senses, leaving her in a pleasant haze that caused her to miss the storm warnings Ramsey was broadcasting so vividly.

"Suggested," she replied, "insisted, even forced. It doesn't really matter anymore, does it? I did the program."

His autocratic silver eyebrows arched over cuttingly cold gray eyes. "Oh, I'm well aware of that. I choked on my coffee this morning while viewing it. I had to change my shirt and tie!"

"I'm sorry," she answered, "they can't all be perfect gems."

"Perfect?" He half rose in his chair, fingers spread on the polished surface of the desk as he pushed himself up. Suddenly, Noel noticed the vein at his temple distending with the increased volume of his blood pressure. "It was an unmitigated disaster! Plus some other more suitable, descriptive phrases which I shall refrain from using only because I've always considered you a lady. That's the reason I'm not repeating some of the more colorful things Jason Merrill had to say about your performance!"

Her shoulders slumped, worry lines etching across her high forehead. "Mr. Merrill saw the program?"

Eyeing her crestfallen expression, Ramsey grew calmer, seeming to wind down from his initial, uncharacteristic outburst. Putting a curb on his temper, he answered on a long-suffering sigh.

"Noel, wouldn't you think he'd want to watch the star quarterback of a team he's spent eight years of his life and millions of dollars trying to bring here? Didn't you think the man just might have a passing interest? Do you want to know what he thought?"

It was obviously a rhetorical question and Noel declined to answer, a fretful frown on her face that was at odds with the almost perfect symmetry of her features.

"What in the hell did you think you were doing? Were you getting back at me for booking McCormick on your program without consulting you? Or"—he paused dramatically for effect, she realized—"were you getting back at Steve Banning?"

Noel sprang from the chair as if shot from a cannon, her hands clenched into tight fists at her sides, her fingernails carving half-moons into the flesh of her palms. "That's unfair!"

His steely-gray gaze held hers, insisting she answer the question truthfully. She lowered herself slowly back onto the cushioned leather, looking down at her lap as she responded softly. "I honestly don't know, Ramsey. I suppose I might have."

He combed a perfectly manicured hand through the lush silver waves of his hair. "Great," he muttered, "now what do we do?"

He removed a gold cigarette case from his suit jacket pocket, extending it toward her as she gratefully accepted one of the long, filtered menthol cigarettes. He took one for himself, reaching across the wide expanse of mahogany desk to light hers before turning his attention to his own. His motions were slow and deliberate, as if they had silently agreed to stall for time, allowing things to cool down a bit before continuing on a more rational level.

Noel worked to pull together her scattered senses. She hadn't been herself since the news of Ross's appearance on her show had been dropped on her. The one thing that was consistent about Noel Heywood was her poise. And her ability to keep a firm grip on her emotions. And her life. Something she'd definitely been lax in the past few days.

Finally, Noel looked up at Ramsey, her expression hopeful. "Did you watch the entire program?"

Ramsey expelled a long breath, the bluish haze of smoke veiling the space between them. "Are you kidding? As soon as you started in on that college versus the pros garbage, I jumped in the car and raced down here. I tried to call first, but the lines were busy."

Her eyes grew as wide as a frightened cat's. "All of them? At seven-thirty in the morning?"

"At seven-thirty in the morning," he confirmed dryly. "It's turning out to be your best-watched program of the year. The switchboard lighted up like a Christmas tree the second you began accusing him of a wild, sexual life-style and was still flashing when I arrived. We had to put some of the early-morning news team on phones since the other two operators don't come in until nine."

Noel rubbed a hand wearily across her eyes. "Oh no." Looking up at him imploringly, she asked, "Does it matter that Ross forgave me? That he said he actually enjoyed himself?"

He sighed again, exasperated with the entire problem. "I don't know, Noel. They're down compiling the calls now. I already know what Jason thinks. Let's not go off the deep end until we discover what your viewing public feels about your display of bad manners."

There was a long, heavy silence as they both sat gazing out of the gleaming glass windows to the desert below. The houses spread out across the flat landscape in neat little rows, filling in the once-barren, desolate floor with families. Families, she considered, inhaling silently on her cigarette, that quite probably held her immediate future in their hands.

Did they have any idea how powerful they were? She had struggled hard for six years to achieve the modest level of success she now held. And at that exact moment, all she could do was sit there impotently waiting for the morning's telephone votes to be tallied.

She jumped slightly as the walnut box on Ramsey's desk buzzed, shattering the expectant silence that hovered over the room. As he pushed a button, Noel was able to hear Kim's disembodied voice enter the room.

"Mr. Scott, Debbie's here with the figures you requested."

He gave Noel a long, significant look. "Here we go," it said. "Thank you, Kim," he replied in the direction of the smooth wooden box, "you may bring them in."

Kim's obviously sympathetic glance toward Noel only served to make her feel even worse, and she could only manage a shaky little smile in return.

Ramsey seemed to be taking his own sweet time as his gray eyes raked the page, studying the columns of printed numbers.

"Well?" Noel asked, unable to stand the suspense a moment longer.

"Why don't you read it yourself?" He pushed the paper to her across the polished desk top. She reached for it gingerly, almost afraid to touch it.

Her strained, taut features slowly relaxed as she read. Finally, replacing the paper on his desk, she looked at him with incredulous, wide hazel eyes. "I can't believe it! How in the world did this happen?"

He grimaced, accompanying the dry look with a lifting of his navy shoulders. "Women. You figure them. Let's face it, Noel—you two were a hit. They consider you one of the most sensational teams since Donahue and Marlo Thomas. Hell! Since Tracy and Hepburn! You managed to make him into a sex symbol, and if that doesn't get the females out to Merrill's stadium, I sure as hell don't know what will!"

He picked up the phone. "Kim, get me Jason Merrill," he said into the intercom line. Looking up at Noel, he asked, "Are you still here?"

She put out her cigarette and grinned, feeling at least a thousand years younger. "Just leaving, Boss."

She was at the door when he called to her. Turning, she faced him questioningly. "Yes?"

Ramsey covered the mouthpiece of the phone with one palm. "You squeaked by this time, Noel. Don't you ever pull a fool stunt like that again! You might not be so lucky."

She offered a brief salute, clicking her high heels. "You've got it, Boss."

She shut the heavy door behind her, leaning against it for one long moment while she caught her breath. "It's all right," she said, looking up to see an anxious

Kim viewing her warily. "I've still got my job and the calls were unbelievably positive."

The young woman exhaled a long sigh of relief, pushing her dark bangs back from her forehead with long, plum-tinted nails. "I'm so glad, Noel," she said sincerely. "Ross McCormick's so absolutely gorgeous, I couldn't understand how you could be so hard on him. I would've been putty in his hands."

Noel looked at the rapt expression on Kim's pretty face, realizing that this was undoubtedly the effect he had on all women. Hadn't even she faltered when faced with the devastating effects of that charm turned on full beam?

"I know what you mean," she confessed. "I think I was fighting it so hard, I used a little overkill."

"I'll tell you one thing," Kim replied, shaking her sleek black hair over one shoulder. "If I were ever in a room with that man, I sure wouldn't waste my time fighting with him!"

Noel smiled understandingly as she left, her step lighter as she approached the elevator. By the time she'd descended the nine floors and returned to the newsroom, relief was in the air. Everyone was smiling at her, evidence that her good news had already broken. It crossed her mind, not for the first time, that if the KSUN news team could uncover outside intelligence as rapidly as they assimilated station gossip, they'd put all the networks out of business.

Despite the best of intentions, she didn't get a lot of work completed as the long hands inched agonizingly slowly around the faces of the clocks on the newsroom wall. Noel knew what time it was in all the world's capitals, yet none of the clocks pointed to the hour she was awaiting. As she glanced up for the umpteenth time, she broke into a welcoming smile as Ross's broad frame entered the room at precisely two o'clock. Viewing him from across the room, she admitted to herself that he was undeniably attractive.

His russet hair was a bit longer than stylishly popular, brushing softly against the collar of his shirt. His eyes were a tawny brown, hooded under wild, uncombed brows. The full beard framing the tanned face curled in a range of colors from auburn to a darkened, burnished gold, and she shivered deliciously as she remembered the soft, springy feel of it against her cheek.

His muscled, hard chest and strong arms molded the light wool of his shirt, forcing the material to take the shape of his body, but the broad upper torso narrowed to a slim waist and hips, encased in soft denim jeans.

His eyes smiled with recognition as he spotted her and headed across the room, his stride unmistakably athletic.

"So this is where you work," he said, glancing around as Noel gathered up her purse and tucked the last of her papers neatly into a desk drawer. "And here I thought you'd have your own executive suite. Especially after our program this morning."

She grimaced slightly at the memory of those cliff-hanger moments in Ramsey's office. "I'm lucky to have a job, period, after this morning."

His deep, throaty laugh caused her heart to pound a little faster as he put his hand lightly on her back and walked out to the car with her.

"I don't believe it!" She stood staring at the sleek black Porsche parallel-parked neatly next to the curb, behind a parking meter.

"I told you I'd do it," he answered, bending his tall frame to unlock the door for her.

Just then her eye caught something she'd missed at first glance. "You cheated! You still didn't put any money in the meter." She pointed accusingly at the bright red metal flag.

He grinned, looking so incredibly boyish her heart did a series of flips. "I was afraid if I turned over an entirely new leaf, you'd get bored, having nothing to work with. I decided to leave you with a bit of a challenge. Reform should never come too easily."

Noel slid into the bucket seat, swinging her long legs gracefully into the car before looking up at him. "Whatever gave you the idea I'd want to reform you?"

"Doesn't every woman yearn to remake man to her own, romanticized ideal?"

Ross closed the door with a soft click and went around in front of the car. Leaning over to unlock his door from the inside, she didn't answer his question, but instead asked another as he maneuvered his long body into the small interior of the sports car.

"Are you in need of reforming?"

He'd slid the key into the ignition, but he didn't immediately turn it. Instead, he turned toward her teasing, smiling face. His toasty-brown eyes surveyed her with great gravity as he touched her cheek lightly with his knuckles.

Forgetting that she'd been hating this man only hours before, forgetting that she was sitting in a car directly outside her office building, forgetting everything but the warm, intimate look he was giving her, Noel reached up and ran her palm down the side of his face, delighting in the feel of his flaming beard against her skin.

His lips moved to feather her face, his warm breath wafting against her eyelids, then her cheeks, following the delicate line of her jaw. She admitted to herself that this was what she'd been waiting for, this was what her body and her heart and her soul had been seeking since that first kiss in the garden the night of the party. After a time, she turned her head so the moist, parted curve of her mouth met his. It was a kiss of exploration, slow and deliberate, as if time had stopped and there was no need for any hurry.

Her head was spinning as his warm mouth moved down to her throat, the mobile lips nibbling deliciously at her tingling skin. She gasped slightly as her pulse leaped in response to his whisper-soft caress.

"I'm incorrigible," he murmured against the throbbing tattoo of her bloodbeat. "Are you by any chance applying for the job of reforming me?"

His teasing, probing lips were creating a warm, euphoric rush of sensation, and her spiraling desire caused her to respond recklessly.

"I might be," she breathed as his lips moved down the V neck of her blouse. She twisted in the bucket seat, to pull him closer, and the silky material pulled to one side, allowing his mouth access to the soft curve of her breast rising above the lace of her midnight-blue bra. "Are you taking applications?"

He gave her one last soul-rendering kiss before returning his attention to the forgotten key dangling in the ignition. "Honey," he answered in a ragged voice as the engine leaped to life, "I'm willing to take anything you're offering!"

The rosy glow left by his kisses was like an opium mist about her head and she leaned back against the soft seat. Her left hand rested lightly on his thigh as they drove in comfortable silence.

He walked her to her apartment door, his long fingers linked with hers as naturally as if they'd been doing so for years. His hands moved to circle her waist.

"See you at eight," he promised, punctuating his words with short kisses.

"Oh yes," she breathed.

"I can come in and help you dress," he offered, his massaging fingers playing havoc on her spine.

"I don't think so."

"Then you're sending me away."

Noel nodded, opening her lips to allow him to deepen the kiss. When she could feel every slender bit of resistance ebbing away, she pulled her head back, moving her lips to rest against the triangle of skin at his collar and delighting in the taste of his warm skin.

"If you ever decided to change careers," he murmured, reclaiming her lips, "you'd make one helluva football coach."

She leaned back a little to look up into his slumberous dark eyes. "What do you mean?"

"If you can actually send me away, when I'm so happy just to be holding you in my arms, you've got to be the toughest lady I've ever met. In fact," he avowed, nibbling at her full lower lip, "you've got to be the toughest person—man or woman—I've ever met. With the possible exception of most professional football coaches. I think, however, you could make the grade. Do you eat nails for breakfast, too?"

Her fingers were playing in the thickness of his hair as she eyed him with mock chagrin, her dark lashes fluttering exaggeratedly.

"Oh, dear. Is that a requirement?"

"Absolutely."

"Well, I've only progressed to tacks so far. But I promise to work on it."

Ross grinned, the corners of his eyes slanting ever so slightly. "Why do I halfway believe that?" He reached up to take her hands from around his neck and place them at her sides. "And now, I'm going to follow instructions and go home. Before I refuse to listen to you and follow my instincts."

He kissed her chastely on the forehead before turning away with a huge sigh and heading down the hallway. His hands were thrust deep into the pockets of his denim jeans as he whistled a merry tune under his breath.

Noel entered the apartment on a golden cloud that dissipated the moment she entered the kitchen and viewed the two cups resting on the counter top.

That morning Ross McCormick had literally pushed his way into her apartment, uninvited and most certainly unwelcomed. He'd displayed every arrogant, hateful male trait she'd been studiously avoiding for years. Now, only a few short hours later, she was practically issuing him a gilt-edged invitation to spend the night.

The insinuation had been there when they'd been standing at the door, and she'd done nothing to discourage it. In fact, she'd done very little to discourage him since the moment they'd met. Including that infamous kiss Friday night, which had broken open this Pandora's box. She might bluster a bit and deny the effect Ross had on her, but he was certainly a man of enough experience to recognize her wanton willingness.

Noel sank down onto the couch, covering her anguished face with both hands. My God, she'd allowed—no, encouraged—him to make love to her right in front of her offices, where she was assumed to be a professional newswoman, not some brazen football groupie! She was infused with self-revulsion as she realized that that was undoubtedly how Ross viewed her.

Ross probably saw her as one of the hoards of available women who was more than willing to cast aside all tenets of decent conduct, just to make love to a famous man. Correction, have sex with a famous man. Because that compelling primitive sensation sparking continually between her and Ross had nothing to do with love. She was behaving no better than those swarms of females she'd had to fight her way through to get to Steve. And she knew all too well what he'd really thought of them.

They'd been nothing but ego boosters. Just like the weights they used to build those strong, steely muscles, men like Steve Banning and Ross McCormick used women to build and sustain their enormous masculine egos. She paced the room, arms wrapped around herself, rubbing her skin briskly for comfort. Finally, after two hours of self-recrimination, she went to the telephone and punched the buttons with a vengeance, as if striking Ross instead of the little Lucite squares.

"Noel! Would you believe I was just sitting here thinking about you?" The pleased, deep voice drifted over the wire and Noel steeled herself to reject its insinuating warmth.

"No."

"What?"

"I said," she repeated frostily, "no. I wouldn't believe that."

There was a long silence on the other end of the line. When Ross spoke again, his voice held a strange, unreadable inflection. "Why are you calling, Noel?"

She drew a deep breath, then rushed the words out in a hurry. "I just called to apologize. I've developed a terrible headache and I'm going to have to take a rain check on that dinner." Her voice rose to a high pitch as the excuse spilled out, almost cracking on the last words.

Again that incredibly long silence. Noel could almost hear the wheels turning in that treacherous, quick mind.

"Have you taken some aspirin?"

"Yes," she lied, "but they're not doing any good. I'm afraid it's a migraine, Ross. But, maybe some other time. I'm sorry."

She was rushing to hang up when she heard his voice bark a harsh order. "Don't you dare hang up, Noel, or you'll have me at your door before you know what's happening."

She lifted the receiver back to her ear, swallowing convulsively. "I really don't feel up to—"

"Noel, do me a favor. Shut up." His smooth masculine voice overrode her. Not harshly, but the threat was there in the low tones. Once Ross was assured by her quick intake of breath that he'd gotten her full attention, he continued.

"We have a date for tonight and I've a hunch you're beginning to have second thoughts about that. So you're pulling the time-honored tradition of a feminine headache."

"It's not—"

"I don't really care," he advised her. "Let me explain how it's going to be. I'm arriving at your door at precisely eight o'clock this evening. Now, if you're dressed and ready to go out on the town, we'll have an enjoyable time with dinner and a show. If you really do have this alleged headache," he warned, his silky voice letting her know he didn't believe it for an instant, "I'll either go out and get something for you to eat, or I'll cook something for you there. Then, I'll tuck you into your chaste little bed—all alone—and leave. And, if you dare to try that other last-ditch excuse, I'll simply spend a pleasant evening watching you wash your hair. In fact, I may even volunteer to brush it dry. Are there any questions?"

"No," she sighed resignedly, "you've made yourself crystal clear."

"Good. Then I'll see you in a few hours. And Noel—" His voice softened to a deep, lush velvet.

"Yes?"

"There's an outside possibility you might even enjoy yourself tonight if you just relax a little bit. Why don't you think about it, okay?"

Noel nodded, the lump in her throat keeping the words from forming. Her hand clutched the receiver as she heard the soft click in her ear when he broke the connection.

6

She felt tugged both ways as she ran the water into the bathtub. Part of her wanted to keep the door locked and bolted. Because Ross McCormick honestly frightened her to death. She'd never known such raw, masculine appeal. That sparkling, blue-eyed charm that Steve Banning had possessed in spades was nothing like this. Now, looking back, Steve appeared absolutely juvenile, small potatoes. And, she mused, pouring in a few shimmering drops of oil from a blue crystal decanter, if she couldn't survive a relationship with Steve, whatever made her think she was ready to be playing in the big leagues?

As she slid into the silken water, leaning her head against the inflated shell-shaped bath pillow, another, more passionate self lurking deep inside her came to the forefront. She luxuriated in the warmth of the soft water as it lapped lightly across her stomach and breasts when she shifted slightly in the herbal blue foam. She imagined it to be his gentle, caressing hands, and her bones grew as soft and pliant as the fragrant water.

She took great pains with her appearance, pinning her hair into an elaborately braided chignon fastened with gleaming gold clasps. She smoothed on some body lotion and followed it with a liberal dusting of talc, leaving her skin dusted with a pearly, fragrant glow.

Noel had loved the whirl of activity of Las Vegas, that Disneyland for adults, when she'd first arrived. Ramsey's frantic social life and high-stakes gambling helped cauterize the gaping wounds left by Steve Banning. But, after the first six months, she became like the child who'd been given the ice-cream store she'd always wished for. Hot fudge sundaes were a delightful treat—once in a while. A steady diet of them paled the pleasure. After a whirling initiation, Noel discovered the same could be said for Las Vegas's nightlife.

This evening, however, she was pulling out all the stops. Slipping on a soft black halter dress, she arranged the plunging neckline, allowing an enticing glimpse of her creamy full breasts. Fastening a stunning, silver sequined-clasped belt about her waist, she stood back to study her image in the full-length mirror.

You're certainly going to a lot of trouble, she told the woman in the mirror, for someone you swore you couldn't stand. Her heart gave a crazy little leap in response to the chiming of the bell and she quickly misted one last touch of perfume, enveloping herself and the room in a seductive, scented cloud of rose and jasmine blended with rich wood scents.

Ross breathed out a long whistle as he stood in her

doorway, brown eyes lighted with lusty approval. "You are the most beautiful creature I've ever seen," he swore, entering the apartment. He leaned his back against the closed door, his hungry eyes practically eating up every satiny, perfumed curve. Then his brow furrowed slightly.

"Is something wrong?" The welcoming smile faded from her lips.

"You are truly beautiful," he avowed, studying her intently. "And truly frightening."

Noel smiled a small, uncertain half-smile, not knowing whether he was teasing her or not. Ross McCormick, who had to face a full line of human mountains every Sunday, afraid of five feet seven inches of nervous female?

"What do you mean?"

"Every time I've seen you," he murmured, "you've looked like something that just walked off the pages of some high-fashion magazine. It makes the average guy a little nervous."

Her hazel eyes were enormous, limpid pools. Ross, an average guy? Never!

"I certainly don't want to scare you off," she replied softly. Her hands reached out and touched his arms, moving to his shoulder blades, her fingers massaging lightly. She could feel the torn muscle and broken bone under her fingertips and the thought of him in pain sent a slight shiver through her.

He'd put his arms around her waist and was looking down into her face with a vaguely speculative look. Then, before she could respond, his hands were in her hair, pulling out the gleaming gold clasps and dropping them to the creamy expanse of carpeting beneath them.

"What are you doing?" she cried out, her hands moving quickly to her elaborately dressed hair.

Ross shook his head, concentrating on his actions. "Don't. Wait just a minute."

"It'll take ages to fix it," she wailed, obeying his instructions in spite of her distress. Her hands dropped impotently to her sides.

"No, it won't. I promise." His strong hands were tangling in her hair, moving adeptly and quickly. When he'd released the glossy, polished chestnut masses from confinement, he lifted the dark clouds, lightly allowing them to drift through his fingertips to settle about her shoulders.

"There. Now you look like a vision who's just stepped from my dreams."

His hands were holding her only lightly, beneath her hair, his thumbs moving against the back of her neck. But Noel could no more move from his desirous gaze than if she were bound to him by bands of forged steel.

He bent and touched his lips to the bare skin shimmering at the base of her throat. "I think you're ready now. Do you want to check—or do you trust me?"

Noel felt his question went far beyond the subject of her hair. That morning in the apartment, and later in the coffee shop, she'd gotten the impression the man could see right through her. That he knew and understood every doubt and prejudice she harbored.

There was a good chance that at the beginning she'd unfairly categorized Ross as a carbon copy of Steve Banning. Ross had seemed to realize exactly what she'd been doing. Oh God, how she longed to trust this man! His touch was causing sheer havoc in her veins and she was tempted, almost willing, to trust him implicitly. But common sense prevailed and she moved reluctantly from his arms.

Going to the mirror, Noel was momentarily stunned

by what she saw reflected back at her. Her hair tumbled in careless profusion, tossing clouds of brunet silk, kissing her shoulders and the bare skin at the top of the deeply plunging neckline. Soft and luxurious, its natural glory had been enhanced. But it was her overall appearance that was so striking. Whereas only moments before she had gazed into this same mirror, viewing an attractive, sophisticated woman, what caught her eye now was the aura of vulnerability and the almost wanton invitation her appearance portrayed.

She was gazing at a woman who very much wanted to be made love to. And the emerald-bright green eyes, pupils expanded with heightened emotion, gave witness to the fact she'd found just the man to satisfy this cresting wave of desire.

Ross had done a lot more than let down her hair. He'd begun to chip away at her carefully constructed wall, lowering those protective parapets that had served her so well for so many years.

She could feel the heat emanating from his body as he appeared in the reflection behind her and they exchanged a long look in the mirror. His expression was as softly gentle and surprised as her own, and he finally broke the spell, shaking his tawny head slowly.

"We're a fine pair," he commented in a husky tone. "All dressed up to go out on the town and still hanging around here. I think we'd better be leaving."

Noel nodded in agreement, relieved he was taking control of the situation. She'd felt as if she'd been floating sensuously out of her depth, and if he'd suggested staying right where they were, she'd have never been able to murmur a single word of protest. And if those beautifully carved lips had lowered to hers, she would have welcomed them, opening under their gentle, nibbling persuasion to offer him the sweetness within. And if those strong hands had reached up to unclasp the fastener of the long black gown, allowing the top of the dress to fall free, granting him access to the perfumed and powdered fullness of her breasts, she'd have only begged him to continue his exploration. As it was, in response to her sensuous thoughts, her nipples were small taut buttons against the silkiness of the fabric.

The man was like rich, dark port, fermented to a robust headiness that made her head swim and her resolve flow away whenever she was with him.

Suddenly, as he shepherded her to his car, she broke out in a bubble of laughter, chasing away the erotic reverie in which she'd been immersed.

"I don't think it's *that* funny," Ross complained. His dark eyes reproved her teasingly, while his mouth tilted in a hint of a smile. He held the bright yellow slip that had been left on the windshield of his car, scowling at it in the mellow glow of the streetlight.

"I do," she said, her words spluttered with laughter. "I kept warning you."

He didn't say anything until they were seated in the car. Then he handed her the parking ticket. "So you did," he agreed. "Would you do me a favor and put this in the glove compartment?"

Noel took it from his outstretched hand and gasped in astonishment at what she saw as she put it away.

"There must be twenty-five tickets in here!"

He shrugged, his attention on the road, the craggy, bearded profile not revealing a thing. "More like thirty," he agreed nonchalantly.

"You'll get arrested!"

He shook his tawny head. "No, I won't. I save them up for about a month. Then I go down and pay 'em.

The guys at city hall all know me. They get autographs for their kids, and a lot of money goes into the coffers of the Las Vegas city government."

She turned to him, her eyes wide. "Wouldn't it be better to simply park where you're supposed to?"

Ross reached out a broad hand and ruffled her hair.

"It would," he agreed cheerfully, "if they'd put parking spaces where I needed them. But, since they don't always, we've got a little system of our own that works real well."

"I don't believe you!" Once, in a blue moon, Noel Heywood could be caught jaywalking. That was the extent of her trifling with the law. Such flagrant behavior, never minding that it only dealt with parking tickets, was totally beyond her comprehension. She knew she'd never be able to sleep with all those yellow slips resting in her car.

Before replying Ross turned the sports car into the long, curved driveway of Caesars Palace, stopped in front of the entrance then handed the keys to the uniformed parking valet before replying. Putting his hand lightly about her waist, he turned her toward him and stopped for a moment as they approached the doors.

"*Believe* me," he stated firmly, his tone suggesting that he was not referring to the parking tickets. "I want you to know you always can." His face was creased with concern for a long moment until it split into the more familiar roguish grin, and they entered the luxurious casino-hotel.

Caesars Palace is world famous for its opulent splendor, built on the foundation of brightly colored chips lost by unlucky gamblers on the green felt tables. Noel knew the dinner she ate and the show she viewed in the magnificent room were probably the most extravagant she'd experienced for a very long time. Yet, if anyone had asked her what she was eating, or who was singing from the spotlighted stage, she would not have been able to say.

From the moment she'd entered the lobby under the spectacular crystal chandelier, her attention had been riveted on Ross—on the smallest of details. On the reddish-gold hair glistening on tanned wrists below the shirt cuffs as he buttered his soft sourdough French dinner roll. On the way the little lines fanned out from his tawny eyes, attractive creases that widened when he smiled at her, which was often. And on the slight scar that cut across the bridge of his nose, obviously a souvenir of his rugged life-style.

Noel watched his full sensual lips move in the framework of the ginger tones of his soft, curling beard and finally, as they sat in a quiet corner of a cocktail lounge hours later, she gave in to her impulse and reached up to trace the cut of those lips with her fingertips. They moved under her touch, kissing her finger. Then he took her hand in his and kissed each of her fingertips—one by one—his eyes never leaving hers.

"That was one of my best ideas," he murmured, his voice husky as dark eyes burned fever bright.

"What?"

"Having Jason book me on your show this morning."

Two things struck her simultaneously. First, could it have been only this morning? It seemed like an eon ago. The second was his suggestion that he'd been the one to plan his appearance on *Wake Up Las Vegas*.

"Good try," she answered, trying to keep her voice steady while his lips were creating incredible sensations through her blazing-hot fingertips. "But it was Ramsey who booked you onto the show."

"Of course. After Jason suggested it," he replied,

his tongue now tracing little circles on her palm. "But I was the one who suggested it to Jason."

Part of her wished they could just stop talking so she could give herself up to the heady golden sensations he was creating. But another part of her whirling mind was piqued with curiosity. "Why?"

"It seemed as good a way as any to meet you."

Noel's gaze left her ravished hand and rose to his eyes, searching for the truth in their smoky depths. "You wanted to meet me? Why?"

"It's a long story," he answered, his teeth nibbling at the soft inner flesh of her palm.

"I've the time." She gasped slightly at the erotic shock.

Ross sighed. "I was afraid you were going to say that. How can I make love to you and talk at the same time?"

She raised her lips briefly to his. "One thing at a time."

His wide shoulders lifted and dropped with resignation. "All right," he replied. "But remember, you asked for this."

Ross pulled her over against him on the cushion of the darkened booth, allowing her to lean her head on his shoulder as he talked. His lips brushed her hair as he confessed, "I've been watching you since I hit town. I kept expecting to run into you. I do a lot of personal appearances, and I knew you did, too. So . . . I waited. But it never happened and I was becoming afraid I'd never have the opportunity to discover if you were anything like that intelligent, bright and incredibly sexy woman I wake up to every morning."

"Every morning?" she teased.

"Most mornings," he allowed. "I did have to permit a few live, flesh-and-blood women into my life, Noel. I couldn't spend all my time fantasizing about you like some lovesick schoolboy."

Noel suddenly hated the thought of another woman experiencing the gentleness those strong hands could impart, and the warm, sweet taste of his lips. But she knew her surge of jealousy was irrational. Even though she felt as if she'd shared a lifetime with this man, she had to admit he certainly owed no fidelity to a television image.

"Jason and I were discussing my contract when he mentioned the desire to get more women interested in the team. He'd given me the perfect opening, so I suggested your program."

Noel's cheeks burned in the dim candlelight as she recalled how she'd reacted to the news of his appearance.

His low, deep tone continued next to her ear. "I was looking forward to it; then I saw you at that party. You looked so perfect, so startlingly beautiful in person—my color television hadn't begun to do you justice. And when I watched you arguing with that congressman, I was excited to see you were actually living up to my idealized image of you. I've been looking for a woman exactly like you for a very long time, Noel. To finally discover you actually existed was like Christmas coming early this year."

She thought back on their bleak short experience only evenings earlier. "I didn't do a lot to reinforce that, did I?"

"You mean by treating me like you'd rather see my head on that silver tray in place of the chopped liver canapés?"

"I'm sorry about that," she murmured, a dark fringe of lashes resting on pale cheeks as she lowered her eyes.

His fingers cupped her chin, tilting her head so he

could gaze into her troubled hazel eyes. "Let's agree to put the past behind us. All of it."

"I thought I had."

His brow furrowed slightly as he contemplated her intently. "You can't say that truthfully, Noel. Not as long as you've got that lithograph of the winter scene in the bright, cheery atmosphere with which you've surrounded yourself. Knowing about Banning, I understand its meaning. The only thing I don't understand is why you'd want to remind yourself continually of all that. It must have been hell for you."

She turned away, her hands crumpling the small white cocktail napkin. Pulling a cigarette from her black satin evening bag, she fumbled for a lighter.

"I'm making you nervous again."

Noel shook her head, her hair swirling between them in a dark cloud. "Not you. I don't like to talk about those days."

"But you like to remember them," he persisted softly.

She looked across the almost-empty lounge, her misty eyes unseeing. "I don't *like* to remember them, I *make* myself."

"Why?"

She shook her head again, the lump in her throat not permitting her to answer. He observed her eyes glittering with unshed tears, her hands trembling as she drew the cigarette unsteadily to her lips, but he refrained from commenting.

"Would you like to know what people thought of you at that time?" he asked instead.

She turned back in surprise. "I thought you didn't know who I was."

He ran his hand down her hair in a gentle, stroking gesture, his brown eyes incredibly soft. "I didn't know

Noel Heywood was Noel Banning," he countered. "But I knew about Noel Banning. We all did."

"Great," she groaned. "That makes me feel just dandy, Ross."

"May I continue?"

Noel inhaled deeply, wishing she could have another drink. A double this time. But the cocktail waitress was laughing as she took an order from a rowdy group of conventioneers and seemed disinclined to look Noel's way. So she nodded, giving Ross her permission. Another drink would only postpone the inevitable pain, anyway.

How could she, of all people, have found herself sitting here with someone so capable of reopening all those old wounds of long ago? She'd thought she was healed, but the past few days had demonstrated there were still a few old hurts festering somewhere deep within her. And not only could Ross McCormick make those worse, he could be capable of inflicting an entire series of new ones. She'd already had proof he was the one in control in their relationship, and if he wanted to take them to a point where she could be harmed once more, Noel didn't know if she could call a halt to it. What was she? Some kind of masochist? Seeking the same type of man over and over? You'd think the fiasco with Steve would have taught her something. She shouldn't have come to Las Vegas. She should have gone directly to someplace where they practiced self-flagellation. Where she'd fit in.

"I'd been in the pros for five years when your—when Banning—was drafted," Ross began. "I was lucky. I didn't have to start immediately the way he did. I was able to get my head out of the clouds and my feet on the turf before having all the media attention riveted on me. I don't know how I would have responded under the conditions he was subjected to."

"Wrong," she answered in a flat monotone. "You were a Heisman Trophy winner your senior year at Nebraska, so the press was already focused on you. And, although you didn't start until the fourth game when Al Monroe was sidelined with an injury, you finished with a winning season. . . . I read some of the articles this past weekend," she answered his astonished look. "But, even if you'd done badly, I can't see you responding the way Steve did."

"Probably not," he answered, surprising her somewhat by agreeing. "Especially if I'd been lucky enough to have someone like you beside me."

He kissed her lightly before continuing, and a sob escaped from her, against his lips. He held her close for a few minutes, as if comforting a small, unhappy child.

"There are a lot of guys who fold under pressure, Noel," he continued. "In the NFL the pressure is all there—and you're trying to live your life in a damned fishbowl. Some players begin drinking and seeing how many women they can score with. Others become religious zealots and there are those who strike out at anyone and everyone because it's too painful to admit that after all those years of working and dreaming about a professional career . . . they just don't belong there. It was your tough luck to get tangled up with a guy who couldn't handle it. Anyway," he said, his voice softening, "I had a couple of friends on the Lumberjacks that year. You know what they had to say about you?"

"No." She stubbed out her cigarette, keeping her attention directed to the heavy embossed ashtray.

His fingers grazed her chin, lifting her desolate gaze

to his. Dark eyes were lighted with sudden merriment as he smiled encouragingly at her.

"They said," he quoted, "that Noel Banning was one classy broad."

The humor in his voice as he repeated the colorful description was contagious and she smiled. "And do you think that's what I am, Mr. Football Quarterback? A classy broad?"

Ross leaned down and growled seductively into the shell of her ear. "The classiest, sweetheart." Then his tone grew abruptly serious. "But there's something you've figured out all wrong."

At this change in tone she pulled a little away from him so she could view him carefully. "And what's that?"

"You've decided that because your first experience with a man turned out badly, it was because he was a football player. Honey, Steve Banning wouldn't have been any good for you, whatever he'd done with his life. You were always head and shoulders above the guy and he knew it. It was probably another reason he felt so threatened. He was waiting for you to realize it."

"I don't know—" she murmured.

"That doesn't matter anymore. It's all in the past." His dark eyes glowed with a strange, angry fire. "What *is* wrong is the fact that you're tarring all athletes with the same brush. Including me!"

Anger shook his voice and Noel shuddered with a momentary fear—an instinctive response. But, just as quickly, his tone gentled and he hugged her close once more. "Try to trust me, Noel. Just give us a chance."

He was quiet on their way home, but as she leaned her head on his shoulder, his hand rubbed down her arm, causing a little quiver of delight as it brushed against the fullness of her breast.

"Can you come in?" she asked, her voice hopeful as he stood in the hallway outside her apartment door. His eyes caressed her upturned face, bathing her in their dark warmth.

"I want to," he admitted. "But I'm not going to."

Noel could feel her disappointment taking over the features of her face, pulling her smiling, uptilted lips downward.

"Hey," he said quickly, taking her lowered chin in his hand and raising her head. His lips brushed against hers in a gentle, reassuring kiss. "I said I wanted to."

"Then why don't you?" Noel asked, surprised by her sudden, atypical boldness.

"Because if I came in, I'd want to stay," he answered truthfully. "And it's too soon."

She twisted away from him, turning to insert the key into her door lock. "I'll just bet it wouldn't be the first time you'd enjoyed a one-night stand," she grated.

"Listen to me, Noel," he countered swiftly, his hands snaking out to grasp her shoulders and spin her around to face him. A pinpoint glitter of anger flared in his eyes and she found herself desperately regretting her hasty words.

"I've told you I don't appreciate your dumping me into the same rotten class of garbage as Banning. I know he hurt you and I'm sorry about that. But, if you're going to keep making me pay for his sins, we may as well call this thing off right now!"

She was sorry. He was perfectly justified in his anger. But how could she explain that her distrust was as instinctive as the passion he was able to kindle into a blazing fire within her? She'd lived with the emotion for over five years, building it to a finely tuned response. It was only that other, deep, disturbing hunger that he'd released that made her unable to turn from him as she might have any other interested man.

Noel wanted to give this relationship a chance, but she didn't know how to begin. There'd been only Steve in her life, and he'd swept her up like a whirling dust devil, throwing her back to earth with a jolt when she no longer served his needs. Nothing about Ross pointed to a similar behavior, yet how long had she really known the man? He was right of course. It was too soon.

Ross watched the play of emotions cross her face, his anger collapsing at the confusion in her hazel eyes. "I overreacted," he apologized.

"No." She shook her cloud of glossy dark hair, her eyes slightly glazed with conflicting emotions. "I did. You were right and I'm sorry. I'd really like to try again, Ross."

He clasped her tightly against his hard, muscled chest for a moment, then put her gently away from him. "Spend tomorrow with me?"

Noel nodded, happiness bringing the shining light back into her eyes.

"How about some tennis to start the day out? Then we'll go from there."

"Don't you have practice?"

Ross shrugged. "That's not your worry," he stated offhandedly. "It just so happens we've got an off Sunday this next weekend. You just be up and ready when I knock on this door at nine o'clock tomorrow morning."

"I don't know," she hedged teasingly. "It's not often I get a day off in the middle of the week. What if I want to sleep in?"

"Go ahead," he growled, giving her one last hard embrace. "But just remember, if you're still in bed when I arrive, you'll have only yourself to blame for how I'll take it."

The seductive thought caused her to shiver slightly and she held herself to the hard length of him before finally breaking the intoxicating kiss to whisper goodnight. As she passed by the mirror in her bedroom, she noticed with pleasant surprise that a sensual smile was still curving her lips.

7

"It's been too long!"

Noel laughed, delighted to see him filling her doorway. As hard as she tried to steel her heart against this man, everything about him made her happy.

"It's only been one night."

Ross groaned, reaching out to pull her into intimate contact with him. "The longest night of my life," he avowed huskily. "Up until now my only sleepless night had been the night before the NFL draft." His hands moved down her soft curves.

"I thought we were going to play tennis this morning," she said breathlessly, not doing a thing to stop the glorious movements of his skimming palms. In fact, her own fingers were twisting in the soft russet curls at the base of his neck while her body moved in seductive rhythm against him.

He chuckled, his breath warming her ear. "At least I know it's not exactly your first choice either," he murmured, his lips exploring the contours of her upturned face. "For once, we seem to be in perfect agreement about something."

He pushed her away from him, giving her one quick kiss before opening the door to gesture her through.

"You realize," he leered as she passed him, "that I have a tremendous amount of frustrated sexual energy that's clamoring to be released. For you even to agree to walk onto the same court with me shows incredible daring. Were you, perchance, ever a wild-animal tamer?"

"It depends"—Noel grinned over her shoulder saucily—"were you ever a wild animal?"

Noel was not surprised he was a superb tennis player. After all, he was a professional athlete, and everything about his strong, muscular physique attested to that. What did surprise her was his almost catlike grace as he moved easily about the burnt-red clay court, seeming to possess the ability to turn on a dime. She had not expected such agility from such a large man.

Having grown up in California, she'd had access to tennis courts year round and was a proficient player. On power and speed, he was heads above her, but Noel had developed a strong base-line game and eventually won the second set—seven games to five.

Her victory was short-lived, however, as Ross came back with a vengeance, taking the third set in straight games. While she laughingly refused to jump over the net to concede defeat, she did allow him to bring her head toward him, into his court, for a long, sweet kiss.

Seated with him beside the court, she put her feet up onto a white wrought-iron chair, stretching her long legs out into the autumn desert sunshine. She was somewhat out of breath from her valiant struggles to take one of the three sets from him and was not unaware of his interest in her breasts rising and falling under the thin, damp cotton of her embroidered white dress.

"I knew it," he commented softly.

"Knew what?"

He ran a hand down the length of her outstretched, tanned leg. "I knew you'd have long, beautiful legs, but I was beginning to despair. I was worried we'd be old married folks before you'd see fit to expose them to me."

Noel felt an unbidden flush burn into her cheeks at his casual mention of marriage. "Whatever do you mean?"

His hand remained on her golden-tinged thigh, tracing tantalizing circles before he stopped, squeezing it lightly.

"Every time I've seen you, you've been wearing either pants or a long skirt," he complained. "I finally decided that a tennis court would be the best way to get you undressed without a hassle."

She slapped his hand playfully. "That's why you suggested this?"

"Guilty," he agreed cheerfully. "And it worked."

"You *are* incorrigible!" she laughed.

"Of course. But you're going to reform me, remember?"

Noel shook her dark, glossy head. "I don't think I have enough time. You're a tough case, Ross McCormick!"

His dark eyes held hers for a long, intimate moment. "Oh, you'll have enough time. I promise you that."

Noel looked at him, her gaze drinking in his thick, auburn hair and hooded, sensuous brown eyes. She remembered girls in college falling for a biology professor simply because he'd had eyes like that. Bedroom eyes, they'd called them then.

The sun was glinting on his strong arms and legs, deepening the dark tones of his tan, making the hairs appear to be spun gold. He looked like a bronzed god, and she was enjoying every minute she was spending with him.

"I'm having a good day," he said, startling her once again with his ability to know what she was thinking.

She smiled. "Me, too. I'm surprised," she answered truthfully.

His rusty brows rose in interrogation. "Surprised? I'm not certain I appreciate that. Did you have any doubts I'd be anything but charming?"

"I'd have been a fool if I had, wouldn't I?" she asked, teasing him with a provocative grin.

"That would be the word for it," he agreed pleasantly. "How do you feel about water-skiing on Lake Mead next?"

Lake Mead had been created when a massive dam was erected on the Colorado River, just a few miles outside Las Vegas. Forming one of the largest man-made bodies of water in the world, the dam originally had been called Boulder Dam but was unofficially renamed Hoover Dam in 1931, to honor President Herbert Hoover. Various factions managed to get the name returned to Boulder two years later, which it remained until 1947, when Congress officially named it Hoover Dam. As it stood now, old-time residents comfortably called it by either name, some cantankerous souls insisting upon the original name of Boulder. Whatever it was called, the lake was a popular recreational sight, drawing visitors from at least four adjacent states.

"Are you always so athletic on your dates?" she hedged.

"You don't want to."

"It's a bit late in the year." Although desert temperatures were degrees above the rest of the country, Noel wasn't wild about the idea of plunging into the November-chilled waters of the lake.

"Darn! And here I thought I'd come up with the ideal solution to getting you into a bikini." His rumbling laugh made her realize she'd been set up.

"I see," she remarked. "But the best you would have gotten today, my friend, would have been a full-length wet suit."

His eyes lazily followed the slender curves of her body, his expression hidden by the thick, copper lashes. "I think," he decided finally, "that your body could do wonders even for that."

"You're going to spoil me," she complained, a smile belying her stern words. "And you'll have only yourself to blame. I just might start to believe you if you keep telling me delightful things like that!"

His eyes suddenly grew black and serious. "That's what you're supposed to do, Noel." Then, just as quickly, his expression grew lighter, the tanned face creasing into a grin. "Since I can't get you wet," he said, "how about we just go upstairs and you can feed me lunch."

"Okay."

"I can tell the lady is just bursting with enthusiasm. What's the matter? Can't you cook?"

Noel wrinkled her nose slightly. "Anyone can fix a ham sandwich."

Ross put his arm around her waist in light possession as they strolled back toward the building. "Ah, but do you make it with Swiss cheese?"

"Of course."

"And spicy brown mustard?"

"Is there any other kind?"

"Kaiser roll or rye bread?"

Noel stopped, looking up at him momentarily, trying to guess which to answer. "Rye bread."

He sighed. "Well, I suppose beggars can't be choosers."

She slapped his arm. "You're right about that!"

He perched himself on a kitchen barstool, watching her work as a light breeze filtered in through the open balcony door.

"I think I'm going to go change," she decided, the cool air uncomfortable on her bare legs.

"Need any help?"

She shot him a long, patient look. "You just don't give up, do you?"

"Wouldn't you be disappointed if I did?"

"Probably," she agreed as she left the room.

"Noel?" Ross called through the closed bedroom door. "I just thought of something. I'll be right back."

She heard the outer door of her apartment close before she could answer. Slipping into a pair of cream corduroy jeans and a neutral boat-neck sweater with dolman sleeves, Noel returned to the kitchen just as he walked into the apartment carrying a brown bag.

"What in the world?" she asked, indicating the bag with a tilt of her head.

Ross kissed her on the mouth before putting the bag down onto the counter and pulling out two dark bottles. "Imported German beer. Only thing to drink with a ham sandwich. And just wait until you see what else I bought!" He rubbed his hands together gleefully and plunged them into the bag, pulling out his other purchase. "Kaiser rolls!"

"For someone who isn't making this lunch, you're certainly choosy," she observed dryly.

"You're right. I am definitely not doing my share."

He gave her that familiar, breathtaking smile. "I'll set the table."

"Let's eat out on the balcony. It's such a nice day."

"You're on." He grabbed some glasses and napkins and went to work.

"You know," he commented, taking a long, cool swallow of the dark Bavarian beer and eyeing her judiciously, "you even look classy in jeans. What a woman!"

"You certainly live up to that Irish name," she laughed, color infusing her cheeks. "You are simply full of blarney."

"I'll have you know I've meant every word I've said about you," he protested. "The good ones, anyway. The others were obviously uttered while I was experiencing a temporary fever of the brain."

Noel looked across the glass-topped table at him. "Then you are either still suffering from that fever"—she reached across, placing the back of her hand against his forehead—"or you are extremely prejudiced."

"Perhaps"—his gaze lightly roamed the ground below the balcony, his dark eyes suddenly brightening with hidden lights—"but there's only one way to find out."

"And what's that?"

He took her hand and pulled her lightly to her feet, leading her through the apartment and out the door.

"Where are we going?" she asked as they rode down in the self-service elevator.

"You'll see," he promised. As they walked out onto the sidewalk, he scanned the view quickly, then looked satisfied. "The only way to prove my point is to ask a neutral bystander," he stated, pulling her over to his car.

Noel might have suspected him of staging it—the timing was too perfect. Standing beside the sleek, illegally parked Porsche was a uniformed policeman who smiled in recognition as Ross approached.

"Hiya, Ross," he greeted him. "You thinking of moving into this building? You'll have your own private parking space then."

Ross laughed heartily, the rumbling echoing deep in his chest. "Don't even suggest such a thing, Danny. We both know it'd never be where I needed it. And besides, you wouldn't get your quota of tickets each month without me as your best customer."

The burly, middle-aged traffic cop turned an angry red at the implication. "I've told you," he blustered, "we don't have quotas!"

"Whatever you say, Officer," Ross returned amicably. "I'm in too good a mood to argue today. Tell me something, Danny," he added, changing the subject. "Don't you think this is undoubtedly the most beautiful woman you've ever seen?" Ross put his arm around Noel.

The police officer nodded his graying head affirmatively. "Always have," he agreed. "But don't tell my old lady."

"Mum's the word, Danny, my boy. And you have yourself a nice day." Ross grinned triumphantly at Noel and took the yellow parking ticket obligingly.

"See," he said, handing it to her to put away with the others, "I told you I'd prove it to you."

"You're crazy!"

He kissed her briefly on the lips before heading back into the apartment building. "About you," he agreed, whistling lightly, happily, under his breath.

They spent the remainder of the afternoon pleasantly, maneuvering their conversation deftly through the realms of politics, religion and the various viewpoints of cat and dog ownership.

"How could I bring my Labrador over to visit if you insist on that Siamese cat?" he asked.

"I suppose you'll just have to leave him home."

"Leave Duke home? By himself?" The distressed look on his face reminded Noel of a small boy who'd just lost his favorite aggie in a marble tournament.

"There comes a time in every man's life," she told him gently but firmly, brushing an unruly lock of rich auburn hair from his forehead, "when he must make a choice. You'll simply have to choose between Duke and me."

"That's unfair! Don't women have to make choices?"

"Constantly," she affirmed. "And Hershey stays."

"Damn-fool name for a cat."

Noel shook her head, narrowing hazel eyes. "And I suppose Duke is of royal lineage? At least Hershey makes perfect sense for a chocolate-point Siamese. If you knew anything about cats."

"I can't imagine wanting to know anything about cats," Ross grumbled.

"Well, I can't imagine some big, hulking dog thundering through my apartment."

"And you think I want your cat visiting me?"

"Cats do not go visiting," Noel scoffed. "People come to them."

"Oh, they do, do they?"

"Most definitely." She tossed her dark head with a patronizing air.

Provocation gleamed in his mahogany eyes. "Pretty sure of themselves, are they?"

They were seated on the couch, and as the light argument had progressed, he'd maneuvered her into the corner. Taking advantage of his superior position, his head lowered and his lips captured hers in a tantalizing kiss. Her lips parted under his, and her hands slid down his back, joy singing in her veins. It was an erotic delight of a kiss, his tongue seeking the sensitive corners of her mouth, gently circling her open, responding lips. His warm lips grazed across her cheek, moving to nuzzle her ear, causing her to feel almost faint with pleasure as his flicking tongue explored its shell-like hollow. When he whispered to her, his breath fanned warm, introducing a flowing heat.

"Then I guess"—his words were a soft summer breeze in her ear, the titillating tongue still moving seductively—"I'll have to leave Duke at my place. I'd hate to see him interfere in this marvelous relationship we seem to have going for ourselves."

Noel was filled with a happy, dizzying glow and wasn't willing to accept that anything under the sun could change the way she felt at that very moment.

"We could get a puppy and a kitten at the same time," she gasped, as his teeth nibbled lightly on the sensitive cord at the base of her throat. "Then they'd grow up friends and never realize they were supposed to hate each other."

Ross lifted her body slightly in his strong arms until she was half reclined on the couch, his long length covering hers, his desire making itself known through the soft cotton of the white tennis shorts he was still wearing.

"Now that's what I call ingenious," he murmured, his lips lightly brushing her lids, causing them to close under his feathering touch. "Just like us. You'd have never known you were supposed to hate me if you hadn't had one bad experience with an athlete."

Noel's sweater had worked loose from her jeans and his hands were skimming hot trails of fire across her rib cage, one palm moving to cup her breast. At his inadvertent mention of Steve Banning, her instinctive fear came hurtling back at her and her eyes flew open, dread vibrant in their jade depths.

"Ross," she cried, pushing against his wide shoulder with her palms, "sit up. Please!"

He instantly obeyed her somewhat hysterical demand, confusion shadowing his dark eyes. He raked his long fingers through his flaming hair, his astonished gaze searching her pale face.

"Damn!" His sharp outburst was followed by a string of virulent epithets as he rose abruptly from the couch and strode angrily across the floor. His long strides covered the short space of the apartment in just a few steps and he spun angrily on his heel, his eyes twin coals in an angry face.

"It's him again, isn't it? Every time you begin to relax and let yourself experience some honest emotions, he comes between us and you freeze up!" Noel watched with apprehension as one huge hand curled into a tight fist, pounding itself into his other palm.

"That's not it," she argued softly, unconvincingly.

"That *is* it!" His long finger jabbed the air between them. His intent glare made her uncomfortable and she looked down at her hands, which were twisting ineffectually in her lap.

Noel was totally unprepared for the sudden movement that brought him in front of her, and she caught her breath as she was yanked off the cushions of the couch and held in front of him. His fingers were gripping her upper arms, digging into her soft flesh, as he held them tightly against the sides of her body. His eyes, only moments before warm and caressing, were chips of dark ice as they glinted down ominously into her stunned face.

"Do you keep him around in that frightened mind

of yours for protection?" he asked between gritted teeth, a white line of anger circling thinned lips. "Does he help you to avoid ever succumbing to normal human passion? To feeling like a woman? Do you drag him out whenever you're afraid of responding like this?" His voice had lowered to one of sheer torment as he covered her lips with his mouth. One hand left her arm to clasp the back of her head, bringing her even closer as he took her breath away with the intensity of his kiss.

Noel's mouth parted in a shallow sob of surrender as her lips softened and parted, inviting him to deepen the caress with his bewitching, seductive tongue. Something was shattering inside her, like crystal exploding from a high-pitched sound, and her arms encircled his neck as she went up on her toes, her full breasts crushing against him as she pressed her pliant body to the hard male shape of him.

Like bark pulled from a tree, Ross had peeled away her layers of protection, leaving her vulnerable and open to a surge of passion that promised to devour her. She heard the breathless little moans echoing about them and realized through her inflamed senses that they were coming from her own ravished lips.

She still clung to him, her legs weak, as he reluctantly dragged his mouth from hers.

"I think," he groaned with answering desire to her sensuous movement against his taut body, "we've just had our first fight."

Ross held Noel a little away from him, gazing down into the dreamy depths of her eyes with smoky desire. One strong hand tangled in the thickness of her hair, tilting her head back, as the other delicately traced the contours of her face, as if he were a blind man attempting to memorize her features. His fingertips were like red-hot needles, and she heard the sharp intake of breath revealing his desire as her small white teeth bit lightly into the heel of his hand. His rib cage raised and lowered as he once again thrust his fingers through her thick hair, but as he did so, Noel noticed with some amazement that his hand was shaking slightly.

"I don't know what to make of you," he breathed, his pupils narrowing as he ran his gaze down her length. "You give me the most inconsistent messages of any woman I've ever met."

"Have there been all that many?" Oh God, how she wished she could take back those incautious words!

"Noel—" Ross warned, a nerve jumping along his jawline, just above the growth of russet beard.

"I'm sorry," she murmured sincerely, her emerald eyes showing contrition. "Force of habit, I guess."

"You're forgiven."

His voice was growing stronger and less ragged as he regained his composure. His fingertips skimmed her face and body gently, without making demands, and Noel cupped his bearded tanned face in her palms, raining light kisses over his features. God, she was glad she hadn't chased him away! Her heart seemed to stop beating as his hands went lightly to her shoulders and he put her a little away from him.

"Come walk me to the door."

"Are you leaving?" Regret was mirrored in her wide eyes.

"Capricious as a spring storm," he muttered. Then he laughed a deep, husky sound. "Just for a little while. Long enough for a cold shower. Then I'll be back to take you to dinner."

He had enveloped her lightly in the circle of his

arms, his mouth just inches from hers as he brushed back the errant dark strands of hair from her face with soft fingertips.

"I have to get up early tomorrow," she reminded him.

"And we'll make it an early evening," he pledged. "But I want to end today in style. I thought we might have an early dinner, then dance for a while at the Top of the Strip."

"I'd love that," she agreed softly.

The apartment seemed especially lonely after Ross had gone, and Noel turned on the television for company. She was dressing, one ear tuned to the KSUN evening news, when she heard a report from Jerry Kush, the sports director, which made her drop an earring. She jerked her head toward the picture being flashed on the screen of the portable television in her bedroom. But she needn't have looked. She'd had that rugged, handsome face branded into her mind's eye since the night of the party.

"You skipped practice!" she accused as she flung open the door later that evening.

Ross grinned, his brown eyes lighted with a dancing, teasing twinkle. He appeared absolutely unrepentant.

"You found out. How?"

"How? Don't you think I listen to my own station's newscasts?" She turned on him heatedly as he entered the apartment. "You were fined. For spending time with me."

He shook his head in mock dismay. "I knew I shouldn't have left you here alone. I could've kept you too busy to find out."

"But you lied to me, Ross!"

He leaned his hips against the dining table, his long

legs crossed at the ankles as his gaze approvingly took in her clinging Grecian-styled crepe dress. The one-shoulder design skimmed the soft curves of her body lovingly, his eyes echoing the same sensation as they followed the flowing white material down to the deep slit in the skirt. His gaze lingered on her long legs, caressed in a pair of whisper-soft silk stockings, one of her few luxuries.

"You look beautiful," he murmured, shaking his head slightly as if disbelieving his luck.

"We were discussing your telling me you didn't have practice," Noel reminded him pointedly, attempting to ignore his desirous glance.

His lips brushed her hair slightly as he placed her white jacket about her shoulders. "I didn't say that," he argued softly. "I simply said it wasn't your concern. And it isn't. Today was worth ten times what they fined me."

Noel looked up at him as they descended in the elevator, her eyes mirroring her worry. "If the press finds out you spent the day with me, it'll be a three-ring circus around here."

As he watched the lighted numbers flashing at the top of the elevator door, he judged the time they had remaining before they arrived in the lobby and answered her complaint with a long, seductive kiss, ending seconds before the heavy steel door opened in front of them.

"You're forgetting," he commented lightly, "you're the only member of the press who knows. And you'll never tell."

His liquid chocolate eyes caressed her all during dinner and afterward, as they moved dreamily on the nearly deserted dance floor of the Dunes Tower. The brilliance of the lights spread out on the desert floor below the vast expanse of windows and the sparkling stars pricking the black sky seemed to pale in comparison to the lights gleaming in the golden depths of Noel's eyes as her gaze answered his.

Luxuriating in the feel of his embrace, she swayed to the sweet tones of the saxophone, her senses spinning from the feel of his body moving against hers, the softness of his breath feathering her hair and the words he was murmuring in her ear. Finally, without a word, Ross simply looked down at her questioningly. Noel nodded; it was time to leave.

8

"Are you coming in tonight?" Noel was poised at the door, knowing with every feminine instinct she possessed that Ross would not go away.

"Am I invited?"

She opened the door, moving inside, turning to smile invitingly. "Well?"

Ross took one step behind her into the apartment, then he slowly closed the door. Noel held her breath expectantly as he took her into his arms. She lifted her face for his kiss, and was surprised as those incredibly gentle lips moved instead to feather soft, teasing kisses on her eyelids, which closed obediently under the sensuous touch. The trail of kisses moved up the side of her face to her temple, increasing the warm beat of blood flowing beneath their touch.

Noel reached up, running her fingers through his hair, her own lips pressed into the warm skin of his throat, her soft curves molding themselves to fit his hard male form. A broad hand moved slowly down her throat, continuing along the soft, pearly skin until it ultimately discovered what it had been seeking. Noel breathed a soft sigh of exquisite pleasure as he cupped the soft globes of her breasts, kneading them with an expert's touch. The fiery beard whispered sensuous promises as it teased its way down her warm skin, his lips finally circling the rosy crowns that had hardened at his touch. His teasing tongue drew muffled gasps of pleasure as a desperate, burning hunger tore through her.

Noel welcomed the feel of his knee parting her thighs as their swaying bodies lowered to the plush cream-colored carpeting. They knelt together for a time, their searing fingers intent on sensuous exploration as he slid his fingers along her thigh, exposed by the inviting slit in her long dress.

His touch caused a flood of passion to wash over her like a wild, cresting wave, and she pulled him down onto the soft bed of carpeting, reveling in his hard male shape pressing against her hipbone. Her thighs moved sensuously against his as their hands struggled to remove the restrictive clothing that was between them. Noel gradually became aware of a decrease in his response and forced her unseeing eyes reluctantly into focus.

"Darn cuff link," Ross muttered, noticing her attention. Somehow, the gold fastener had caught on a loop in the creamy expanse of carpeting and held his arm fast to the floor above her head.

Noel sighed, as the sparkling blaze of feeling began to diminish. "Let me see," she said, sliding out from under him and kneeling beside his captured arm.

His eyes darkened to an inky black with regret.

"Let's just rip it," he suggested, his lips reaching up to brush her freed breasts.

Noel felt a definite stirring somewhere deep in her middle regions and she stifled the small cry that had been about to escape her lips at the delicate embrace.

"No," she decided reluctantly, "I think we'd better unhook you."

"I'd rather finish unhooking you," he murmured with a seductive glance. Noel followed his gaze, noting unashamedly that the top of her dress was gathered about her waist and her skirt was twisted, revealing a long expanse of silk-clad thigh.

She managed to free him, but they remained where they were, neither moving to reinitiate their passion-filled lovemaking, or to separate. There was a familiarity that suggested there was nothing else they should be doing but sitting on the floor of her apartment, staring into each other's eyes.

She didn't object as he pulled her back down the rest of the way onto the carpet, stretching his long length beside her as he propped himself up on an elbow. His free hand reached out to brush the tumbled hair back from her face, looping it behind her ear.

"You know that you're driving me insane, don't you?"

"I'm sorry." The liquid look in her emerald eyes denied the words. Noel was thrilled she was able to put that escalating, desperate hunger into those dark brown eyes. The slight trembling of the hand that was stroking her fingertips only proved, without a doubt, that Ross was affected by those same strong forces that had been buffeting her about with all the power of a hurricane-force gale. He might be far more experienced in such matters than she, but he wasn't a good enough actor to fake his responses.

"I don't believe it," he said as he planted a firm kiss on her lips. "You should probably be warned, my lovely, that you're playing with fire. My wild Viking blood is nothing to toy with."

Noel tried to ignore the caressing hand that was circling her breasts and causing her nipples to rise like hard pink rosebuds. She willed her mind to concentrate on their conversation.

"I thought you were Irish."

"That's true," Ross murmured, his head bending to lightly graze her breast with his lips, plucking at the rosy nub. "But my family hails from County Wexford. It was an early Viking settlement," he explained, demonstrating his equity by moving his head to lavish his attentions on her other breast. "When the Vikings landed on the coast, some of them stayed, chasing the wenches, that sort of thing. In my case"—he lifted his head to grin at her wickedly—"some wild Viking managed to outrun a comely young colleen, adding his barbarous genes to the McCormick stock."

She looked at the flaming hair and beard and felt he did indeed resemble a tempestuous Viking warrior. This was a man who rode his emotions hard and he'd need careful handling.

"Are you trying to frighten me?" Noel asked softly.

"Hey!" He clasped her to him, kissing her tenderly, his lips lightly grazing her mouth. "I don't ever want to scare you, honey. Or hurt you. I think I just want to love you."

She shifted in his arms to fit her body against his, her own fingers exploring the hard muscled chest under the crisp white shirt. Her hand moved slowly along his rib cage, and Ross gave a long ragged sigh as her fingers probed past the waistband of his black dress slacks.

"Perhaps," she suggested against his mobile lips, "it was the wench who outran the Viking."

His head drew away for a moment, his hungry brown eyes taking on the richness of velvet as his fingers moved to lower the zipper at the back of her dress.

"Do you think that's possible?" There was a soft hint of pleased surprise in his deep voice.

Noel lifted her hips, encouraging him to slide the white crepe down the long expanse of tanned leg. "Oh, I'd say," she murmured, "that it was quite possible. In fact," she added huskily, rolling over to cover his length with her own, tangling her silk-clad legs with the firm male ones under her, "that it was most probable."

She delighted in the feel of his solid frame under her soft contours, and she moved with instinctive seductiveness against him, her hips clinging fluidly to his firm thighs. His strong hands reached below the waistband of her lacy garter belt, kneading her firm buttocks as he pressed her into his aroused male force. The feel of that hard masculinity against her barely clad body caused a dam to burst somewhere inside of her, the feminine instincts which flowed forth as ancient and intense as the forces that created the earth—an earth which was at that moment tilting wildly and threatening to go spinning out through the universe.

"All right, wench!" There was a half groan, half laugh as Ross pulled her hands from their heated exploration, holding them far out to either side. "You've had your fun. Now it's time for you to learn just how far the fair maiden can tease a barbarian."

"Do you plan to have your way with me?" Noel asked with a soft, breathless gasp.

Ross's eyes were smoldering with unmistakable

desire as he rose from the carpeting to stand over her. He began to undress, his gaze never leaving her face as his shirt fell to the floor beside her, followed in agonizingly slow order by his slacks and then his low, hip-riding briefs.

"I do, wench," he answered finally, mock brusqueness causing Noel to tremble with anticipation.

"Thank God," she breathed, the supple movements of her slender body inviting whatever invasion he had in mind.

Hovering over her, Ross was all leashed power and raw virility and her love-bright jade eyes stroked him, following the fiery hair that curled deliciously as it funneled down toward his navel and beyond. Noel knew her burning desire was mirrored in her eyes, because suddenly their gazes collided, no longer soft and tender but aflame with a hunger that could wait no longer.

It was as if the world had ceased spinning on its axis and the heavens were holding their breath as his knee bent to the floor beside her hip and Noel knew that she would never forget this moment as long as she lived. Whatever happened in the future, wherever her life would lead her—her mind and her body would be indelibly branded with this frozen moment in time.

His fingers scorched the satiny skin of her thigh as he unhooked the silk stocking from the garter belt and slowly unrolled it down her long leg, taking his time, as if unwrapping the most precious of presents. Noel closed her eyes to the unhurried, maddening sensation those fingertips were creating. When both stockings had been dispensed with, Ross's hands burrowed under her hips, unfastening the snowy garter belt with deft fingers. She watched through heavy lids as Ross appeared willing to let her remain clad in the wispy ivory panties.

He extended his long length over hers, keeping himself above her body by the sheer strength of his arms. His lips appeared unable to make up their minds as he kissed her temples, her cheeks, her parted lips. They ravished her throat and tormented her breasts as he systematically branded her nakedness with his searing kisses. While his tongue explored her with a moist torture, his lush full beard caressed her skin with whispers of rapture, and she heard her soft, pleading feminine sounds.

"Ross . . . please . . ." Her hands moved down his back, down the back of the hard thighs, urging him to cover her with his strength.

"Soon," he tempted, his voice a husky promise. "There's just a little bit more . . ."

Noel cried out as his teeth nipped at the skin on her stomach, creating a spiraling warmth she could feel within her as well as without. The springy beard brushed along the inside of her thighs as Ross continued his sensual banquet, taking little bites down one outstretched leg and up the other. His treacherous, darting tongue probed its way under the filmy white material she still wore and roved across her flat stomach, causing Noel's hips to lift from the carpeting in response.

In acquiescence to her mute plea, the panties disappeared, as if dissolving under his touch, and his dark eyes flamed dangerously, making her skin feel as if he'd lighted a torch to her length. At the first contact of flesh against flesh Noel could hear the indrawn hiss of his breath, even over her own muffled gasp of pleasure. The sexual energy that had been crackling about them since that first meeting now erupted into a fierce, full-fledged storm, as if lightning were forking vividly about them, filling the room with a green, sulfurous glow.

The prolonged, practiced assault on her senses had created a fierce hunger in her that she begged him to satisfy. "Oh, Ross . . . my God. . . . I've never wanted anyone like this." She moaned deep in her throat as his long fingers moved to the damp feminine warmth of her, unlocking her secrets with an expert touch. At the same time his stabbing tongue was driving her to the very edge of oblivion. Noel clung to him in wild longing, her fingers digging into the muscled contours of his back.

"You're right, Noel," he groaned, moving between her thighs, locating the center of her warm passion with consummate accuracy. "There's never been anything like this!"

Their bodies moved in fluid unison, Ross holding back until Noel thought she could surely live no longer, such was the desperate fire in her veins. Her body arched with compelling need, absorbing the deep thrusts as she writhed under him. There was a roaring in her ears and her breath tore through her lungs as she exploded into a kaleidoscope of brilliant rainbow colors. They were one body as they rode the golden spiral to touch the sun, fused together into a molten gold eternity. The warm, loved feeling continued to wash over her in waves as she lay there, stunned even through her languid contentment at what Ross had just taught her about her own body.

"Better." His voice was unusually weak as his lips brushed against her temple with a delicate, light feathering. An experience vastly different from the almost furious ravishment.

"Better? Than what?" Her own voice croaked, ending up somewhere between a whisper and a hiccup.

Ross was kissing her again, his lips possessing a

claim to her his body had already ensured. "Than my wildest fantasies." The dark eyes had a wicked, devilish gleam. "I'd always considered myself a man with a vivid imagination, but you've just managed to surpass it."

"Really?" she murmured, kissing him. "And had you imagined this?" Her pink tongue darted out, sinking deep into the lush coppery beard, laving the sensitive skin hidden under the soft curls. "Or this?" Her teeth and lips took turns nibbling at the strong cord of his throat, feeling the pagan beat of his blood increasing its rhythm.

"Noel . . ." he warned on a choked gasp, "I'm not as young as I used to be, babe."

"I know," she murmured, uncaring of the weak protest as her tongue discovered his dark brown nipples and teased them to erect, thrusting little points. "Absolutely ancient." Her lips explored through the soft carpeting of chest hair and she was rewarded with an answering tremor as she blew hot, teasing little breaths into the indentation of his navel.

"Noel!" If it was another warning, it threatened something altogether different as her lips burned a trail down his thighs.

"Had you imagined this, Ross?" Her glittering gaze engaged his dazed one in a sensual little dance before she returned to her leisurely worship of his hard, athletic physique. She took him lovingly, her hair a chestnut curtain in which his hands tangled as her lips caressed Ross with an innate sensuality. With a tenderness born of womanly instinct, Noel loved him in a way that soon disproved his warning, her tongue caressing him as her hands massaged his rock-hard thighs.

With a harsh cry, Ross turned her in his arms, taking

her in an all-consuming whirlwind of passion, groans tearing through his body as he drove her into the cushioned padding of the plush carpeting.

"My God, wanton," he moaned a long time later. "I think you've killed me!"

Her smile was as warm and loving as any a woman has ever shared with a man. "I'd never do that, Ross. Think of all I'd be missing."

"So this is what it all comes down to," he muttered, lacing his hands through the tangled waves of chestnut silk that were spread across his chest as she rested on him lightly. "I'm destined to end my days in sexual servitude."

"Oh?" She raised her dark head to look up at him, hazel eyes gleaming with golden sparks. "You don't like the idea?"

"Do I get to rest sometimes?"

Noel considered the matter. "For short spells. To regain your strength."

Ross laughed. "It's a deal, then." She watched as he seemed to be gathering up his scattered clothing.

"Are you leaving?" Regret was mirrored in her wide eyes.

"You have to work tomorrow morning. Today," he amended, eyeing her antique regulator clock on the wall over their heads. "And here I promised to have you back home and in bed early."

"A promise you almost kept," she reminded him with a grin, eyes agleam with reminiscent pleasure.

"You *are* a wench," he decided. "Wanton, wicked and saucy. And you know what?"

Noel stretched like a luxurious cat basking in the warm sun. "What?"

"I wouldn't have it any other way."

Noel watched him dress, enjoying the sight of the powerful masculine body she'd known so well. "I think this is where I tell you that I had a lovely day. And evening."

"So did I, honey. And you can take that to the bank." Ross grinned down at her, buttoning his shirt. "See you after work? That is, if the wench is willing."

Noel reached out her arms, inviting him to pull her up to join him. She pressed herself against him, burying her head in his shoulder, her lips tracing its bumpy, irregular line.

"This wench is always willing," she said softly, lifting her head proudly, suddenly no longer afraid of the consequences the events of the evening might bring. She'd never felt more like a woman than she did now. Strong, capable and, yes, loved. Something had passed between them that transcended the mere bounds of sexuality. And although neither had put a name to it, it made her feel terrific.

Noel spent every minute she could with Ross during the next two weeks, their relationship moving swiftly forward, love seeming to bloom as openly and freely as the vivid paintings with which Noel had surrounded her apartment.

"Don't you think it's time you took that dreary thing down?" He was standing near her living-room wall, his back to her as she tossed a fresh green salad.

"I've gotten used to it," she replied, her gaze following his to the wintry gray picture.

"It doesn't go with the room." Ross frowned as he looked around the bright lime-green and soft peach tones of her apartment. "It's too dismal. It doesn't fit in."

His hands were thrust deeply into the pockets of his slacks and he was rocking back and forth on his heels as he turned to look at her over his shoulder.

"I spent a lot of money on it," Noel argued, pouring

wine vinegar and oil onto the crisp spinach leaves. She put the salad on the table and filled the flowered earthenware plates with linguine smothered in a rich, red sauce. "Are you coming to eat?"

"In a minute." He reached up and took the picture down from its hanger and moved past her into the kitchen, where he tossed it into the wastebasket she kept tucked away in a cabinet under the sink. "Now I am."

Noel's eyes widened incredulously as she held the salad servers in midair. "Ross! That lithograph cost me one hundred dollars!"

He opened his dark leather wallet and pulled out five twenty-dollar bills, which he laid one by one on the table next to her plate. "Here. Buy yourself another, happier one."

"But, Ross—" Noel continued to stare at him in disbelief.

He reached out to pour her a glass of Burgundy from the carafe on the table, his stern look assuring her that it was the end of the discussion.

"It doesn't belong anymore, honey. Not in your apartment. And not in your life."

"I have to leave town tomorrow," he said later as they watched the glittering lights of Las Vegas's famed gambling casinos blink on and off.

"I know. I'll miss you."

Ross was lying with his head in her lap and he reached up to pull her down to him, kissing her with an intimate familiarity. "I'll miss you," he murmured against her responsive lips. "But I'll be thinking about you."

Noel jerked her head away abruptly, looking down at him with a grave expression. "You'd better not.

You're supposed to be thinking about the game. If you think about me, you could get hurt!"

He grinned devilishly, recapturing her lips, his soft beard feathering her face. "You know, if you're not careful, I might begin to think you cared. And I thought you weren't worried about the plight of us professional quarterbacks." Dark, smoky eyes twinkled with overt laughter.

"That was a long time ago! When I was much younger and not nearly so intelligent."

"Two weeks? That's a long time?"

She nodded, running her hand across his chest. "Forever."

Ross covered her hand with his own, larger one. "Don't worry that pretty head about a thing. I'm a passing quarterback, remember? None of that razzle-dazzle option stuff. I'm getting too old."

"I thought we'd proved that you're not old at all."

He favored her with a reminiscent grin before lifting a broad shoulder in a slight shrug. "I'll be thirty-five Monday. And while it may not be old in the real world, it's getting up there in mine." His contemplative gaze returned to look out over the brilliant trail of gaudy lights. "I don't have my life all planned out with such detail, like you do, Noel. I knew I wouldn't be playing ball forever. That's why I went back to school."

The russet head shook, moving in her lap. "Some of those guys," he continued, "can't ever look beyond the next game. And they end up one day on the sidelines, wondering what the hell they're supposed to do next. I don't want to end up like that. It's time I started making some serious decisions."

"I understand what you're feeling," she said softly, ruffling the coppery hair with her fingertips, "at least as much as anyone who doesn't play football could. But what makes you think I've got my life all mapped out to the letter?"

The head turned, his dark eyes looking up into hers. "You told me that in five years you intend to be anchoring a major evening network-news program. I've watched you work, and I've grown to know you enough in the past two weeks to know you're enterprising enough to hurdle any roadblocks that might get in your way. I've not a single doubt in the world that five years from now I'll be watching you with my dinner, instead of my Rice Krispies."

Noel didn't answer, knowing Ross could probably hear the increased tempo of her heartbeat so near his head. She'd set that goal when it had become apparent that her marriage could never be salvaged. That her future lay in her work, reaching the pinnacle of her profession. That glittering, faraway goal had soothed the pain, working as a mental balm against the crushing weight of heartache.

But the time with Ross had forced her to reexamine her feelings. She realized that as marvelous as these days were, no relationship could remain a golden, frozen moment in time. It either had to go forward or end. And she knew that although she was comparing weeks to years, the imprint Ross McCormick had made on her heart was far deeper than that ever left by Steve. If she had to go through the rest of her life without Ross, looking back on these days, the ache would always be there. And no amount of professional success would ever be able to soothe it away. She'd opened herself up to an incredible amount of pain.

"Hey!" Long fingers smoothed the furrowed lines marring her soft brow. "Let's not be so gloomy. We should be making far better use of our time."

He left the warmth of her lap, then gathered her up into his arms and carried her without a word into the bedroom. Her fingers played with the soft curls at the back of his neck while her mouth clung to his, drinking in his sweet essence, like a drowning person who can only grasp at the life preserver and hold on for dear life.

As they discarded their clothing, Noel was aware only of the growing warmth beginning somewhere deep in her middle regions and spiraling outward until every nerve ending seemed to be flaming with a crackling red glow. Her knees bent in response to the mattress pressing against the back of her legs, and she dropped onto the bed, pulling Ross with her.

Noel moaned with a fiery need as he covered her length with the hard, warm strength of his body, and she moved under his exploring hands, which ran from her breasts to her hips. Her own hands reached out and slid over his aroused body, feeling his muscles tense as he groaned with hunger against her lips.

His lips and hands and tongue roamed her body at their will, searing all the sensitive little hollows, bringing her to the brink of release then backing away, like the cresting of waves on the ebb and flow of the midnight tide. Noel's turn came as she treated Ross to the same sweet torture, exploring the familiar terrain of his masculine body.

"Oh God, Noel . . . Noel." Ross breathed her name hoarsely, the ragged sound of it on his lips causing her to feel as if her blood ran with molten lava as his hands lifted and shaped her hips. She lifted herself up to meet him, her own parched, dry lips murmuring his name over and over in a litany of love.

Their lovemaking surpassed the normal realm of time, and much, much later, Noel could only curl peacefully in his arms, murmuring a soft, loving purr of contentment before drifting off to sleep.

9

Noel didn't know how long she'd slept, but her eyes fluttered open to observe Ross lying beside her, propped up on one elbow as his dark eyes gazed upon her spent, naked body in what could only be described as quiet triumph.

"Hello, Sleeping Beauty," he murmured, running a fingertip down the side of her face, tracing her cheekbone. "I was wondering how long you'd be out like that." His finger curved around the outline of her full, swollen lips, teasing the corners into an upward tilt.

"I'm relieved to see that you need a little rest periodically, too," he chuckled. "I was afraid you were out to sap all my manhood, so you wouldn't have to worry about me ever again."

"I hope I didn't succeed." Noel smiled, running her palm down the side of his face, playing with the crisp, tawny curls of the beard. Her hand curled about his neck, bringing his lips to hers for a leisurely, satisfying kiss.

"Your eyes are almost jade right now," he murmured, smoothing her love-tousled thick chestnut waves behind her ears to allow him to study her eyes more intently. "I thought they looked more turquoise earlier."

"They change," she answered. "They usually go green when I'm angry, or upset, or—"

"Or making love?"

"Is that what we've been doing?"

Noel knew it was a dangerous question. It could cause him to run like the devil out of her apartment and out of her life. But she had to ask it.

Ross's eyes were a velvety brown as they took in her softened features, her gold-flecked emerald eyes, her swollen, love-pinked lips. If there was one thing he wanted to avoid, it was hurting this woman any more than she'd already been hurt. There was a chance that something very important was happening here. But, just as Noel had needed to separate her myth of athletes from the reality of Ross McCormick, he needed to make certain he'd separated the fantasy of that poised, perfect newscaster from the woman herself. One particular part of Noel frightened him. He understood that she'd developed her strong ambition in order to survive the agony of those days with Steve Banning. And in order to succeed, that ambition had grown to immense proportions, almost dwarfing her at times.

He knew that she cared for him a great deal. And their lovemaking was more than any two human beings could ever dream of. Yet, more than once in the past two weeks, he'd gotten that last-minute phone call. He was second in priority to a fast-breaking story.

If the day came when Noel had to choose, would his love be strong enough compensation?

"I don't know," he admitted finally. "I think it might be. But it's happened so fast. I need to sort out a few things." His face creased with concern. "Does that hurt you? That I can't come right out and tell you that I love you?"

Noel reached out, running her fingers along the soft flame beard. "No. Because I feel the same way. And, I've never felt like this before."

"Never?"

"Never," she affirmed. "I thought I loved Steve. When I first married him. But, if this is love, well, I didn't even come close."

He pressed his lips against hers for a long, intimate kiss. "I'm glad. I don't like the idea of anyone else ever having you this way."

A dark brow rose. "Are you telling me you're jealous? With all the women you could have?"

His finger traced her full-blown lips. "Insanely, where you're concerned. It's that wild Viking blood, I tell you," he grinned wickedly. "You just stir it up."

His dark brown eyes left her face to check the time on her bedside anniversary clock as it twirled gracefully.

"I should have become a lawyer in the first place," he said, his lips plucking at hers gently. "Then I wouldn't be having to spend so many weekends on planes. But, when I was making those early-life decisions, who'd have realized there'd be such a better place to spend my time?"

Her smile faltered a little. "Oh, dear. You're telling me you're leaving."

"Gotta pay the rent, babe. They're expecting me to show up with the rest of the team in Chicago."

Noel's hand reached out to make little circles on his chest.

"Stay here and I'll pay the rent," she suggested in a low fluty tone.

He'd risen from the bed to stand beside her, and his hand was allowed one long, leisurely caress, from her throat to her knees and back up again.

"Wench," he charged on a ragged, deep laugh. Pulling the tangled sheet from the bottom of the bed where it lay in a discarded ball, he drew it over her. "Now cover yourself, or I'll never leave. And every sportscaster in the country will find out you're responsible for the Lobos taking to the field without a quarterback."

Her liquid green eyes drank in every strong masculine feature, as if memorizing every inch of him for the duration they'd be apart. It would be three days before she would see him again. An eternity.

Ross dressed, then sat back down on the edge of the mattress. "When I get back," he promised softly, looking into her unhappy face, "we need to have a long talk."

"Be careful," she whispered, leaning forward to brush his lips with her own. Then, after he'd left and she'd heard the door close, she whispered, "I love you."

Just saying it aloud brought the truth home. She did. Noel Heywood, avowed hater of all professional athletes, most of all football players, had fallen undeniably, wonderfully in love with Ross McCormick, star quarterback. And what was even more amazing was just how ecstatic the realization made her feel. She hugged her pillow to her breast, wondering how she was ever going to sleep alone in her bed again.

* * * *

She managed to get through the weekend, only really feeling alive as she listened with her heart in her throat as Las Vegas took a razor-thin victory from Chicago. At the Lobos' win, she breathed a deep sigh of relief as Ross finished the game without an injury.

When Ramsey unexpectedly showed up at her door, she was grateful for the company, greeting him with a welcoming smile.

"I've got good news for you," he said without preamble.

He sat down on the flowered couch and took the drink she offered him. His gray eyes were silvered and the muscles quirked about his mouth as he observed Noel with his best cat-that-ate-the-canary expression.

"I can always use good news," she smiled at him. She'd already had her share that day. It had been nice that the Lobos had won the game. It was even better that Ross had not gotten hurt. But the superlative news was that he'd be home that evening. Since he'd entered her life, it seemed as if she were on a roll. Every waking moment was perfect.

"We're going to New York tomorrow."

"Tomorrow?" Ross was returning tonight. His birthday was tomorrow. Noel certainly wasn't about to go anywhere now! Not when she'd promised that all-important, serious discussion. The one she prayed would bring a proposal.

"I can't," she answered simply.

"Of course you can," Ramsey overrode her brusquely. "We'll rerun some of your more popular shows, with promos during the week for anyone who missed them the first time around. It'll work out fine. Barry will handle the newscast."

"All week? How long were you planning on being away?"

"*We*," he corrected, "will probably be gone five to seven days. I've got some important meetings with the network brass."

"Why do you need me?"

His eyes lighted with triumph. "I was wondering when you'd get around to asking that. Remember those tapes we sent? Well, they want to meet you. Dan Mitchell, one of the myriad of vice-presidents in the news division, asked me to bring you back with me."

Her eyes were emerald saucers. "Do you think they're really interested?"

He lifted a cashmere-clad shoulder in an elegant shrug. "They'd be crazy if they weren't. I always knew it was only a matter of time before the network boys latched onto you with their greedy, talent-grasping hands. You're a natural, darling. And I would guess they must be interested or they wouldn't have asked me to bring you to the meetings. They've seen the tapes. That they want to talk with you is an encouraging sign. It sounds to me as if you've already cleared the first hurdles."

Noel rubbed her forehead with her fingertips, furrowing her brow slightly as she did so. "It does sound that way, doesn't it?"

Ramsey looked at her in obvious surprise. "You certainly don't sound very excited," he complained. "I thought it would be all I could do to keep you from spending the night at the airport, waiting for the plane to take off."

Wrinkling her nose slightly, she smiled at him. "I am terrible, aren't I? I was just thinking about Ross. And what to do."

"Do about what?" There was a genuinely confused expression on his patrician face.

"I don't know if I can leave Las Vegas right now."

He gave her a severe look under the smooth silver

brows. "I can't believe I'm hearing this! There can't be that much between you two yet. Not the way you were fighting only a couple of weeks ago."

When Noel didn't answer, he asked, "You're not telling me he proposed?" His tone was incredulous, and she felt slightly embarrassed by his attitude.

"No."

He breathed a long, patient sigh. "Well, then," he remarked encouragingly, "there's not one reason in the world why you shouldn't go to New York. Since he hasn't proposed, and the network hasn't offered you a job, I'd say that perhaps you're borrowing trouble."

Noel stood up, offering a ghost of a smile. "I think you're probably right," she agreed. "But I should call Ross and let him know I'm going."

"Fine. You do that. And I'll pick you up about six tomorrow morning. We've got an early flight."

After she'd seen him out, Noel realized that Ramsey's view was the most practical. She and Ross hadn't made any firm commitment, after all. It did seem, in the glaring light of reality, that she was perhaps assigning more depth to their relationship than it allowed. And if their feelings were as deep as she thought, the relationship could surely survive a few days apart. Besides, she hadn't questioned Ross's need to go to Chicago for this game. How could he object to her work taking her out of town? And she'd make his birthday up to him.

She called his hotel but was told that he'd checked out that morning. Remembering that he'd mentioned his flight departed shortly after the game, Noel forced herself to wait an appropriate amount of time before beginning to call his apartment. By two o'clock in the morning she'd packed and repacked twice, cleaned out her refrigerator, washed her hair and read one hundred pages of a latest best-seller, of which she could not remember a single word. She had also called his apartment sixteen times, only to receive no answer but that of a machine, saying he wasn't at home. She finally fell asleep in a chair, not waking up until Ramsey rang her bell at five-thirty.

"What time is it?" she asked groggily, her eyes hazed from too-little sleep.

He looked down at her nightgown-clad body, his raking glance taking in her sleep-tousled chestnut hair, his firm mouth compressed tightly in disapproval.

"For your sake, it's early. You're not ready," he accused, as if she'd overslept on purpose.

"I'm packed," she rushed to assure him, her dull, drowsy mind beginning to come to life. "And I can be showered and dressed in just a few minutes. How much time do I have?"

He pushed back a snowy-white cuff to observe a slim, understated but extremely expensive gold watch. "You have half an hour," he decreed.

"No problem," she promised, running toward the bedroom. "Would you be a dear and make some coffee while I shower?"

"I'm not a servant," he protested haughtily.

Noel turned in the doorway. "It'll help me wake up so I can move faster."

"In that case," he replied, moving toward the kitchen, "hurry up."

She was in and out of the shower in seconds, wrapping a large peach terry towel about herself as she sat down and hurriedly began applying her make-up. She could hear the ineffectual sounds of Ramsey banging about in her kitchen, obviously ill-prepared for domestic work.

"I can't find the filters for the coffee maker," he complained, calling out to her.

"Look in the top cupboard."

"I did."

Noel knew without a doubt that she could march in there, open the cupboard in question and see the box of white paper filters directly in front of him. But that would take more time than they had.

"Then make instant. The jar's next to the range."

"Instant?" His tone left no doubt that he considered the prospect totally unattractive.

"For heaven's sake, Ramsey. Put on the kettle, boil some water, put a spoonful of coffee in a cup and stir! How difficult can it be?"

"That's easy for you to say," he retorted with autocratic dignity. "You're a woman!"

She shook her head in exasperation, stabbing her eye with the mascara wand. Dabbing at the tears with a tissue, she thought how lucky it was for Ramsey he was wealthy enough to pay people to do these menial chores for him. He'd probably starve to death, otherwise.

"You did it!" Ramsey nodded with approval as she joined him. She took a sip of the coffee he handed her, grimacing at the bitterness. What had the man used for a measuring spoon? A snow shovel?

"Just one more thing to do," she assured him, picking up the phone and pushing the familiar numbers which, after the previous night, her fingers could maneuver automatically. "Ramsey." Noel turned to him, her voice shaky. She was beginning to be very concerned. "There's no answer at Ross's apartment."

"So?"

"So, his plane should have been in last evening." Her lips trembled with her trepidation. "You don't think the plane could have crashed or anything?" Her hazel eyes were shadowed with escalating distress.

"Of course not," he assured her swiftly. "If any airplane carrying the entire Las Vegas Lobos football team had gone down, don't you think I'd know it? It would have come over the wire and we'd all be either out in the field or down at the studio, covering the story. We're in the news business, remember?"

He was right. As usual. But then where was Ross? All she kept getting was that damned recorded message. And she didn't want to leave as personal a message as hers on some machine.

"I'll try again at the airport," she decided, deep lines creating slash marks between her gently curved dark brows.

"Do that. And don't scowl that way. Those wrinkles are not what the network's looking for in women newscasters."

"Chauvinists," she muttered, picking up her purse and moving to the door, allowing Ramsey to take the suitcases.

"Not really," he returned smoothly. "Have you really looked at Brokaw or Rather? They're almost as good-looking as you."

"I liked Walter Cronkite just fine."

"But he's gone," Ramsey reminded her.

"I know. And I cried when he said good-bye. He left me without a role model." She slid into the cab Ramsey had waiting, not bothering to consider what it had cost while she'd been showering and getting dressed.

"Since you're into athletes these days," he advised, a wicked smile crossing his distinguished features and looking out of place, "you might try Howard Cosell."

He ducked deftly as Noel swung her slim black purse at his head.

"Noel. That's our flight they just announced."

She covered the mouthpiece of the pay phone with one hand. "I still only get a recording, Ramsey."

"Then, leave a message and hurry up. That's what he has the machine for."

She sighed, her desperate eyes moving around the terminal, as if to find an answer scrawled somewhere on the walls.

"You go ahead, Ramsey. I'll catch up."

"No way. We're both going. Now."

She felt terribly self-conscious, with the impersonal machine and Ramsey both waiting for the message. Taking a deep breath, she rattled out, "Hi, Ross. Noel. I'm in New York. Have a happy birthday. I'll call you." Should she add love? To a machine? She couldn't do it. She hadn't yet said it to him in person. And Ramsey's hovering countenance didn't help. "Bye." She practically shouted into the phone as Ramsey took it from her hand and hung it up.

There were so many people to meet and so many impressions to make that Noel kept busy the entire seven days she and Ramsey were in New York. It was as if she were operating on auto pilot, she considered grimly, during a brief respite from her whirl of interviews. She had still not spoken with Ross. It was as if he'd disappeared from the face of the earth. Everytime she called his apartment, all she heard was the mechanical voice on the answering machine. She knew he was all right. She'd made Ramsey check with Jason Merrill. *Why wasn't he answering her calls?*

Although she kept picturing every moment she and Ross had spent together, rerunning the scenes continually over and over again in her mind like an all-night movie theater, she still managed to smile at the right times and say the right things to the people in New York. Noel knew the attitude of the network people was approving and she began to realize she was being considered seriously for a network spot. Ramsey was nothing less than thrilled with the way things were going. Noel wished she, too, could be as elated.

When the offer finally came, the final day, she waited until they were on the plane to confide in him. She'd been worried that he'd insist on remaining in New York an extra day. To paint the town. And she had to get back to Las Vegas and track down Ross McCormick!

"So, we'll be losing you." He toasted her with the champagne he'd ordered from the flight hostess immediately upon being told the news.

Noel ran her fingernail along the rim of the glass. "I don't know. Probably." She refused to meet his irritated glance.

"Probably? Don't tell me you didn't give them an answer!" He thrust his fingers through the thick, silvery waves of hair and it occurred to her that there had been very few times in their relationship when she'd witnessed the unflappable Ramsey Scott struggling for self-control. And this most definitely was one of those rare times.

"I told them I'd like to think about it," she told him, her hazel eyes rising to observe him calmly.

"They must have thought you were crazy!"

She held his astonished gaze with a longer, sober one of her own. "No," she contradicted, "they understood I need time. I have a few days to make a decision. And even if I decide not to accept, it's been wonderful just to have been offered the chance."

"Well, *I* think you're crazy. Does all this have to do with Ross McCormick?"

"Yes," she answered, the bright light in her eyes warning him not to attempt to dissuade her. "I think I owe it to him to discuss the options. It would be tricky, but not impossible, for me to take this job and continue our relationship."

"Owe? Relationship?" Ramsey shook his elegant head in exasperation. "You don't owe the man anything! And as for your relationship, I haven't seen him jumping to return that constant stream of telephone calls you've been sending westward."

She took a sip of the champagne, eyeing him over the top of the glass. "It's still my business, Ramsey. Whatever you think. I'm not running away. Not this time."

She resolutely ignored Ramsey's attempts to dissuade her from discussing the offer with Ross. She knew that the decision was, in the end, hers alone to make. Yet, she felt certain that Ross still held an important place in her life. Their attraction had blazed from that first, angry spark, yet what they felt for one another had to be more than simply sexual attraction.

She phoned the number which was now emblazoned on her brain the moment she arrived at the airport, for once being saved the frustration of the mechanical answering device. The droning of the busy signal, however, was not a balm to her tense nerves. She didn't bother to go into her apartment as the cab dropped her off in front, opting instead to throw the poppy-red suitcases into the backseat of her Mustang and head the car in the direction of Ross's building.

10

She was practically holding her breath as she rang the bell to his apartment, quickly mumbling her rehearsed speech under her breath, afraid to trust herself to just blurt out whatever popped into her head. But her carefully chosen words flew from her brain as the door opened and Ross appeared, clad only in a pair of jeans, his hair slightly rumpled and his feet bare. Ramsey had a penchant for early-morning flights and Noel had not taken into account the difference in time flying west, plus the fact that Ross had played a game the day before. She'd obviously gotten the man out of bed.

"Hello, Noel," he greeted her with indifferent calm.

"Hello, Ross," she answered, a tiny catch to her voice betraying her discomfort. She ran her fingers lightly through her dark hair, the gesture an attempt to give her trembling hands something to do. The action caught his interest and his brown eyes were unreadable as they took in her glossy, dark chestnut hair, pulled away from her face with two tortoiseshell combs and allowed to fall loosely in soft waves down her back.

The pastel tones of her pink blusher and lip gloss, plus her confusion, made her eyes appear to be a delicate, gentle turquoise, and his dark gaze lingered there for a moment, as if he were trying to read the secrets deep within. His impassive face softened instantly, then slid back into the cool mask. Usually radiating a calm self-assurance, Noel now gave the impression of graceful fragility.

She took a deep breath, deciding to plunge into the obviously icy waters. "I just got back from New York and I thought we might talk." Her soft eyes held a slight pleading and she could feel him relenting. Just a little.

"Come in," he offered, moving aside so she could enter.

The first time she'd seen his apartment, Noel had been struck by its bright, friendly atmosphere. She'd expected leather and dark colors—traditional masculine furnishings. But Ross seemed to be a constant study in contradictions, any attempts to pigeonhole him doomed to failure. Bright and breezy, the apartment walls were a gleaming white. White couches and easy chairs made up a comfortable seating arrangement, using a white brick fireplace as a focal point. Tall palms were placed in strategic corners about the room and the white bookshelves were filled. A black and white steerhide rug resting on the soft white carpeting and the rich patina of dark wood were dramatic touches. The only evidence of his sports life was an enormous LeRoy Neiman painting, framed in modern metallic gold, placed over the fireplace. Capturing the rugged essence of football, the signed painting seemed also to capture the soul of Ross McCormick.

Today, however, she noticed none of this, her attention on the occupant of the friendly, cheery apartment. It was scant consolation that he looked as miserable as she felt.

"I woke you up," she apologized softly.

He only shrugged in return.

He certainly wasn't going to make it easy, she determined, forging ahead anyway. "You look as if you could use some coffee," she offered, moving away from the door and toward his kitchen.

He followed her, dropping his somewhat aggressive stance. "Do you know how much time I could save every morning if I could figure out a way to take this stuff intravenously?"

She laughed, scooping the measured coffee grounds into the basket and pouring the water through the automatic drip coffee maker. "You could always snort instant."

"It's a thought," he agreed, slumping into a chair, as if every bone in his body were grateful.

Noel pulled out a chair and sat next to him, eyeing him judiciously. "You look like you're more than tired. Rough game yesterday?"

"Too much Scotch last night," he corrected. "You'd think I'd know better, wouldn't you?"

His dark eyes rose to meet her gaze and Noel noticed the little tracings of red veins in the usually vivid whites. She'd never seen him drink hard liquor.

"Since when do you drink like that?"

"I started last week, celebrating my birthday here alone." The wide shoulders lifted and dropped in a careless shrug. "Then I discovered what Xylocaine does for my shoulder a steady diet of Scotch does for the rest of me. Numbs the pain."

This wasn't going at all as planned. Noel escaped the room for a moment, locating some aspirin in the medicine cabinet. She took a deep, calming breath, trying out faces in the bathroom mirror until she found one to her liking. There. That looked far more self-confident than she felt.

She shook out two tablets from the white plastic bottle, then poured him a glass of juice from the pitcher in the refrigerator.

"Start with these," Noel suggested.

Ross looked at the glass she was holding out to him and reached for it, surprising her by circling her wrist instead with his long fingers. Pulling her lightly to him, he settled her down onto his lap, his lips nuzzling at her neck.

"Why are you all of a sudden being so good to me, I wonder?" He moved aside the collar of her blouse to let his tongue trace the hollows of her shoulder bone. Her hands were against the warm muscled wall of the bare chest and she could feel the steady beat of his heart under her fingertips.

"Coffee," she murmured, as his lips traced indelible paths on her throat, erasing every coherent thought she'd arrived there with. God, how she'd missed his touch! It had been as if all week her skin had been deprived of some calming substance in the air.

Ross allowed her to get up and pour the coffee without a word of protest. Throwing the aspirin down his throat, he flung his head back to swallow the orange juice in a long gulp. Noel watched the movement of his Adam's apple in the tanned column and wondered why even that was capable of causing the restless fluttering in her nerve endings. When his eyes returned to meet hers, his expression had successfully slid into the impassive mask. He took the coffee she offered, eyeing her curiously.

"I thought you came by to talk."

Her network offer! It had been driven completely from her mind!

"I tried to call you all last Sunday night," she began. "Finally, Monday morning at the airport, I had to leave a message on your recorder. Did you get it?"

He nodded. "I did. And you couldn't get me Sunday night because the airport at Chicago was fogged in. I had to spend the night in the terminal."

"Oh. I called you from New York, too."

"I know."

"You didn't call back."

"Was I supposed to? You never asked. Just told me you weren't able to come home yet. I figured that out for myself. Even being the dumb jock I am."

"Ross, what's the matter?" She lifted her head to exchange a long glance with him, and Ross could observe the tired blue shadows under her eyes that the carefully applied makeup hadn't quite hidden.

"Nothing, Noel."

She wasn't buying it. Not for a moment. Hard as it was proving to be, Noel pressed on.

"Why are you angry with me?" she asked, a quiver in her soft voice.

Ross expelled a long, weary sigh, and he rubbed the stubborn jaw. "I'm not angry. Not anymore."

"But you were?"

He nodded, a brief duck of the tawny head. "For a time. Don't worry about it now, Noel. How was your trip?"

"They offered me a network spot. As a news correspondent."

"Where?"

"That's what's interesting." She offered an uncertain little smile, encouraging him to be pleased for her. "They're trying a new concept of Sunbelt coverage.

Traditionally, they've centered their stories on both coasts—New York, Los Angeles, with Washington D.C., of course. And some emphasis on the Midwest. The rest of the country has been more or less left to roving correspondents and local stations."

"But the flow of population and money is to the South," he inserted, his expression absolutely inscrutable.

At least he's paying attention, she encouraged herself to continue.

"Exactly. They're going to operate a new bureau out of Houston. It's a big, vibrant, growing city and it's centrally located to the states both east and west of it, all which are experiencing rapid growth."

"So, you'll be moving to Houston."

The studied nonchalance was beginning to get to her, and Noel pulled a cigarette from her purse. Lighting it, she ignored his narrow-eyed look of irritation. Noel knew very well that Ross didn't like her to smoke. She'd actually stopped again, early in their short-lived relationship. When she'd calmed down and trusted him, and believed that he cared for her.

After the first comforting breath, she watched the ring of filmy smoke grow larger before saying simply, "I don't know. I told them I needed some time to think about it."

He placed a chrome ashtray in front of her, his face still an impassive mask. "Is it a good offer?"

"I think it is."

His broad, bare shoulders lifted in a shrug. "Then, what's to think about?"

Noel realized with blinding clarity that he didn't care one way or the other whether she took the job or not! The fact that she would have to leave Las Vegas meant nothing to him. In fact, they were discussing this as if there had never been any feelings between them at all. As though they were simply two strangers, sitting on a bench, waiting for a bus—chatting to pass the time.

She ground out her cigarette angrily in the ashtray, noting with some small satisfaction that she'd scattered gray ashes on the polished gleam of the table.

"I guess nothing," she snapped. "In fact, it's a wonderful opportunity, and I can't wait to leave this town and go on to bigger and better things!" She was on her feet, turning toward the door.

A twitching muscle in his jaw hinted at Ross's struggle for self-control.

"Noel," he said on a deep, low tone that was revealingly unsteady, "sit down."

"All right." She was more than happy to take his advice. Her legs had all the consistency of warm Jell-O at the moment and she slumped into the chair. There was a long, significant silence, as if they both were gathering strength, and finally Noel leaned forward, her elbows on the table, her chin cupped in her palms. Her eyes were somber as they held his equally unhappy gaze.

"I need to know, Ross."

"Come here." The husky invitation, instead of warming her as it once would have done, frightened her. Whatever Ross was going to tell her, from the rueful expression, she didn't think she was going to like it.

"Why?" It was a whisper.

"Because I want to hold you."

God, that was what she wanted! More than anything. This man had wreaked havoc with both her body and her mind and she had to figure out where she stood with this wonderful, impetuous man who'd stormed into her peaceful world and changed her life. With the suicidal instincts of a moth flinging itself into the flame, she rose, moving to settle onto his lap once more, her arms circling his neck.

He shifted her on his thighs, encouraging her head to rest on his shoulder as his hands stroked her back.

"When I started out in the NFL," he began softly, "I was drafted by the Rams. But you knew that."

"Yes."

"I packed my bags and left Nebraska with the strength of a man and all the emotional maturity of a naive farm kid. I met a young actress, who was as beautiful as she was talented, and I thought I'd just become sole owner of the Great American Dream. I had everything a big, dumb kid could ever want. We were married after a week."

"And then?"

"And then we spent the next three months fighting over whose career was going to come first. All the Rams had me doing was playing second-string quarterback. The only time I ever got to go out on the field was to punt. It was making me crazy, but when the rumors began circulating that I was going to be traded, I couldn't wait to leave town."

"But the actress?"

Noel could feel the wide, broken shoulder shrug under her cheek. "First she laughed. I mean, she couldn't believe I'd be stupid enough to expect her to give up her career for a football player."

"But you did."

"Hell, yes. I gave her an ultimatum. You know, the old woman's place is with her man. Wither thou goest, stuff."

"I'm sure she appreciated that," Noel murmured into the warm skin of his shoulder, seeing the fireworks that must have ensued between the two ambitious individuals.

"She hit the roof," he agreed wryly, the tone indicating that he'd been naive to expect anything else. "I was traded back east for a running back, a first-round draft choice and two players to be named later. It was a great deal for me. I'd be a starter."

"That's when the marriage ended?"

"The divorce papers came a few weeks later, catching up with me in time for the play-offs."

Her fingers traced the line of the soft red beard. "I'm sorry, Ross."

"Don't be. A few months after we split, she married a big producer and her career took off. And, I did all right for myself. But the episode taught me an important lesson."

"And that was?" Noel felt a tremor of fear skim up her spine.

"You can't expect people to change their lives. Their goals. Just because it'd be nice for you. It's unrealistic."

"But—"

He put his finger over her lips. "No, Noel. This isn't the time. I don't know what I'm going to be doing next year. And in truth, neither do you. You're on your way up, honey. That's why I thought, when I got back from Chicago and found you off chasing your rainbow, that it was a perfect time for a nice, clean break. Before we both get hurt."

Her distressed hazel eyes moved across his face, wanting to reject the message she read in every deeply etched line. It should have helped that his complexion was gray with fatigue, letting her know that this wasn't any easier on him than it was on her. It wasn't fair. They hadn't been given enough time.

"It isn't fair," she objected softly.

Ross shook his russet head, giving her a hard kiss

she had the horrible feeling would be the last she'd ever have from him. Then he slid her off his strong thighs, taking her hand as he walked her to the door.

"Life isn't always fair, honey." He lifted her trembling chin with one finger, compassion touching his eyes as he observed hers, sparkling with unshed tears. "Hey." His fingers traced her upper lip, pulling them into an upward curve. "It'll be okay. In a few weeks you'll be the nation's media darling and have everything you ever wanted. And you'll thank your lucky stars you didn't throw it away for an aging jock with a bum shoulder and a newly acquired propensity for Scotch."

Noel rested her head on the padded steering wheel of the Mustang for a long time, mustering up her strength to drive home. She'd been given plenty of evidence that Ross McCormick could be maddeningly stubborn, but this was a first. She couldn't believe he was right. But that thrusting jaw could just as well have been carved from granite, and he'd obviously spent the week making a decision he was refusing to put aside. The only thing left for her to do was to try to throw herself back into her work and assuage the pain she knew would overwhelm her when this icy, numbing shock began to wear off.

Not wanting to telephone the network offices in New York from her own office, Noel made the call from her apartment. She forced enthusiasm into her voice as she accepted their welcome, offered by Dan Mitchell. She stopped in cold horror as the conversation continued from his end.

"Of course, Dan. It's a great idea. I'll get on it right away," she confirmed in a cheery voice she managed to dredge up from somewhere. Once she heard the click from the New York end of the long-distance line, she slammed down the cream-colored receiver, causing the phone to jangle in response.

"I'm going to murder Ramsey Scott!" she yelled to the four walls of the apartment before storming out.

Noel ignored the frankly curious stares of the news staff as she angrily strode across the newsroom to the wall of elevators on the far side, her high heels making harsh, staccato clicks. A door opened obediently to her strong pressure on the button and, stepping inside, she broke a pink-tinted nail as she jabbed her finger onto the number nine for the executive suite.

"Don't bother to warn him," she told a stunned Kim as she marched by. "I'll announce myself!" The blazing fury in her green eyes assured the secretary she'd brook no denial to her order.

Ramsey was seated behind his wide desk speaking on the telephone, his back to the door, when Noel stormed into the office.

"All right," she shouted, her hands on her hips, "how could you do this to me?"

Ramsey swiveled around slowly in his high-backed leather chair, eyeing her mildly, not a flicker of disturbance on his sophisticated features.

"Gerry, I'll get back to you later on this," he said into the mouthpiece of the phone before placing the receiver into its carved, walnut-boxed desk case.

"Now," he addressed Noel suavely, "what seems to be the problem?"

"I called the network just now," she answered through white, taut lips.

"You took the job, I hope."

"I did."

His face broke into a genuine wide smile. "Great! Where shall we celebrate?" From the way he was rubbing his hands together, Noel could tell he was clearly pleased.

She placed both palms on the polished surface of the desk and leaned menacingly toward him. "I'm not certain you'll be alive long enough to celebrate anything!"

"Noel, what's the matter?"

"The matter? Ramsey, whatever possessed you to send the McCormick tape to the network?"

His gray eyes lighted with sudden comprehension. "Is that what all this is about?" He pushed a button on the intercom. "Kim, would you be a dear and bring Noel and me both a cup of coffee?"

"I don't want any coffee!"

"Well, I do. And I hate to drink alone." He observed her with amused indulgence. "Now, why don't you sit down and we'll discuss this like two reasonable adults."

Her cheeks burned at his inference, but she obeyed, settling herself into a chair directly behind where she stood. Leaning forward, she extracted a cigarette from the ivory case on his desk.

"You really should cut down on that," Ramsey scolded gently.

"Look, I've been told that enough lately. I don't need it from you. If I want a lecture about my smoking habits, I'll call the surgeon general."

"I was only concerned about your welfare."

"My welfare? How can you sit there and tell me that? After what you've done?"

The door opened and Kim entered, eyeing Noel cautiously from beneath her sleek, black bangs. She brought the coffee over to the pair at the desk, but Noel was in no mood to smile, so she kept her eyes down, murmuring a soft "Thank you" as Kim handed her the dark, rich brew.

"Thank you," Ramsey seconded. "Oh, Kim, one more thing?"

"Yes, Mr. Scott?" The young woman turned from the door, where she'd been about to make her escape from the icy tenseness of the room.

"Hold my calls until Noel and I finish our little chat, will you?"

Kim's dark eyes were impassive, displaying once again, Noel observed, her aptitude as an executive secretary. Although she probably knew more than anyone in the company what went on under the KSUN roof, she'd never been known to whisper a word of rumor or an innuendo of gossip. Noel realized Kim was probably consumed with curiosity—she was only efficient, not a saint—but she also knew the young woman would never display one bit of personal interest in her boss's concerns. Noel hoped Ramsey appreciated her and paid her accordingly.

Kim's voice, as Noel expected, revealed nothing. "Of course, Mr. Scott. Just ring if you need anything."

When they were alone again, Noel demanded, "Why did you send that particular tape?"

Ramsey lifted his hands slightly in a shrug of a gesture. "I don't know. I wasn't planning to. Then I thought about all those positive calls. So, at the last minute, I tossed it in. Didn't they like it?"

She sighed, realizing he hadn't meant to create such a dilemma for her. She should have known better. As usual, Ramsey seemed only to be acting in her best interests.

"They loved it."

A crease of puzzlement furrowed his tanned brow. "I don't understand what you're so upset about."

Noel heard a rattling noise and glanced down to see her cup shaking in the saucer. Placing both on the desk, she reached for yet another cigarette and lighted it, forgetting the one that already rested in the ashtray. She inhaled deeply, taking as much of the burning but somehow soothing smoke into her lungs as she could.

"Ramsey," she stated, speaking very slowly and deliberately, hesitating slightly between words. "They loved the interview with Ross." She had to push his name past the painful lump in her throat. "They liked my football knowledge and think the male audience might accept the fact I understand the game while the women would enjoy my point of view. A feminine look at the sport, so to speak."

To Ramsey's credit, he never once looked as though he'd lost his grasp on things, although at that moment Noel knew him to be confused. It wasn't unexpected. She considered how stunned she'd been when Dan Mitchell had suggested the assignment in the first place.

"Ramsey, my dear, well-meaning mentor," she continued, a dry tone to her voice, "we seem to have a phenomenon on our hands here in Las Vegas. The Lobos are headed into December undefeated. Do you have any idea how remarkable that is?"

He shook his head.

"Well, Dan Mitchell does," she muttered. "And, he thinks it would be just peachy keen if I were to cover the team while they remain on this winning streak. A close-up glimpse at the Super Team."

"And that, of course, includes Ross McCormick."

"My goodness, you are fast today," she snapped sarcastically, then immediately was apologetic. She twisted a long strand of dark hair. "I'm sorry, Ramsey. It's just not turning out to be my day."

His keen eyes softened. "Have you spoken with McCormick?"

Noel nodded, unable to meet his concerned gaze. Pity was one thing she didn't think she could handle right then. In fact, she'd been feeling a lot better when she'd been angry as hell. She was beginning to feel sorry enough for herself without Ramsey compounding her depression.

"I take it he approved the move?"

Her slim shoulders lifted and dropped defeatedly. "He did. He calmly explained all the reasons why our relationship could never come to anything."

"Noel, I'm truly sorry. Is there anything I can do?" He reached across the desk to cover one trembling hand with his own, patting it rather ineffectively, as if uncomfortable with the extremely personal turn the conversation had taken.

She looked up at him, her full lips quivering slightly as her eyes brightened once more with those hot, unshed tears. "You can give me the rest of the day off so I can go home and have a good cry."

"You've got it," he replied instantly. "Would you like some company later? I can take you out to dinner."

She shook her glossy head. "No, thanks, Ramsey. I got myself into this condition. It's up to me to get myself out."

"May I tell you he's probably right? The entire affair was just too young to sustain such a separation."

"You can tell me," she said, experiencing a sharp stab of pain at the word he'd chosen to describe her love for Ross, "and he can tell me. But I think it'll be some time yet before I'm able to believe it."

There was a Pacific storm system moving into Las Vegas, bringing with it a warm, gentle rain. Noel opened the arcadia door to her balcony and sat in the apartment, glumly watching the steady drizzle. The usually brilliant desert sky was a heavy slate color, the gray of the inky clouds as dismal as her mood. It crossed her mind that the weather—and her feelings—

for the first time in weeks matched that wintry painting Ross had thrown away.

It was her own fault, she scolded herself as she sipped a cup of fragrant herb tea. She should have kept her distance—not rushed in so impetuously.

But a little voice in the far reaches of her mind argued, Ross had seemed to be rushing in just as fast. They had been like two freight trains on a collision course.

She could only hope that once the stabbing, blinding pain in her heart dwindled down to a steady, dull ache, she would be grateful it had worked out this way. What if she had turned down the network to remain in Las Vegas with him and he'd decided later to break it off? Then it would have been all for nothing.

Not completely nothing, the insistent little voice echoed. You would have known a delirious love while it lasted.

Aha! "While it lasted." That was the definitive phrase. No, it was better to be out now. Before it got even more painful.

More painful? the voice inquired persistently. Could you feel any worse?

No, she answered it, salty tears falling into the dark amber depths of the tea, I don't think so.

11

During her remaining two weeks at KSUN, Noel tried to keep her mind on her work, not counting the days until she would be leaving the station to begin her coverage of the Lobos for the network. It occurred to her in one wild, hopeful moment that if the team were to lose a game before her two weeks were up, the story would die a natural death and Dan Mitchell would have to come up with a different assignment for her.

The first Sunday she remained in her apartment while the Lobos played across town. She listened to the home game that afternoon, discovering it was difficult, in fact, downright impossible to root against Ross.

The second Sunday the game was out of town and was broadcast as the television game of the week. It was then that she knew for certain she was still hopelessly hooked on Ross. Every close-up was an agonizing experience as she watched his coppery hair spring into thick curls that glistened with perspiration. Even through his face guard, she could view his dark eyes, and her memory recalled those intimate moments when those same eyes, now intent on calling plays, had smoldered with desire for her.

When the offensive team came off the field with a comfortable lead in the fourth quarter, Ross pulled off his helmet and grinned at the close-up camera focused on him. Noel felt as if her heart had suddenly stopped beating. It was impossible to hate him. No matter what happened, she was still in love with him. And always would be.

The next morning Noel met with Rob Fletcher, the cameraman sent to Las Vegas to work with her. He was a longtime member of the network news team, now slated to be making a move to Houston. She was thankful for this early opportunity to become acquainted with him. It would make things less strange when she herself made the move to Houston.

He was a friendly, dark-haired man, with arresting clear blue eyes and a ready smile. Tall and lanky, he reminded her somewhat of a young Jimmy Stewart, with his lean, angular frame and easygoing attitude. That attitude, she was to discover, successfully camouflaged a tremendous capacity and love for his work. He'd been with the network for fifteen years, he told her, spending the first ten of them in war-zone coverage around the world.

Noel knew he was a professional from the word go, and was relieved he was the one chosen to break her into this work. She shuddered at what it would have been like if she'd been assigned a neophyte like herself. Talk about the blind leading the blind! Whenever she had time to think about it, those old familiar butterflies began fluttering their wings against the inside of her stomach.

Jason Merrill greeted her warmly as she and Rob were ushered into his office, immediately dispelling her initial nervousness. He shook hands heartily with Rob and surprised the younger man with his familiarity with a Cambodian-refugee series for which Rob had received a filming award.

They had a lively session, Jason practically bubbling over with enthusiasm over his football team. When compared with some other owners, Jason didn't seem to give two hoots about the business aspect of the Las Vegas Lobos.

"I knew the key to the franchise was Ross McCormick," he informed Noel with unrestrained glee. "Too much challenge was gone from the game for the boy. Heck, four Super Bowl rings, all the records he'd set. He was giving serious consideration to retiring. But I knew the idea of building an entirely new championship team—from the ground up—would appeal to him!"

Which it had. Jason had already lured a renowned college coach away from a mid-central team by enticing him with the warm desert sunshine. Armed with the coach and Ross for a quarterback, he'd then gone shopping, managing to sign most of the players he'd been seeking. Eventually the rest were acquired through skillful trading of the expansion players granted him by the NFL.

"Some call me the man who's going to ruin football, with my excessive salaries," he told them frankly. "But I tell those detractors to look at the interest created by our team. When we show up in a city, you can guarantee a sellout crowd. I'd like to know how that's hurting football. And Ross—even without the money, the boy'd be the best quarterback in the country. And without our team I doubt if he'd still be playing. How good would that have been for the sport, do you think?" he demanded into the lens of Rob's camera, bright blue eyes blazing with righteous indignation.

They went out to the field to watch a practice and Noel refrained from interviewing the players, saving her short air time for the coaching staff's opinion of the team's amazing season. Her presence was acknowledged by a sprinkling of good-natured wolf whistles from the players, but if Ross noticed her, which she was certain he must have, he showed not a flicker of recognition.

"We going to feature McCormick today, Boss?" Rob asked five days later. Noel had been well aware of his puzzlement as she'd continued to ignore Ross's presence on the team, finding ways to work around the star quarterback. She also knew Rob had been getting anxious, knowing the network would soon be unhappy with their joint effort if Noel didn't change her tactics.

"In the first place," she stated firmly, "we both know I'm not your boss. If either of us were to be given that distinction, it would have to be you. You're the one with all the experience."

"Ah," he argued, picking up the minicam, "but you're the beauty. Can you imagine the network putting me in front of a camera?"

She watched as he pushed back a shock of black hair from a high, prematurely lined forehead. Perhaps he wasn't the most handsome man she'd ever met, Noel considered, but Rob Fletcher was certainly one of the nicest. He'd proven himself invaluable to her, and it was time to put aside her fears and to stop endangering his career as well as her own.

She was relieved when Ross didn't treat her any differently from any other newscaster sent to cover the Lobos. Although he was cooperative and friendly, there was nothing to indicate they were anything but casual acquaintances. Their whirlwind affair seemed no more substantial than a desert mirage. There were even times that Noel could almost believe she'd imagined the entire thing.

She'd been on her new job just one week when Ramsey insisted on throwing a party to celebrate her success. If there was anything Ramsey Scott loved, it was entertaining, and he was opening up his lavish desert home for the occasion.

Noel chose a simple but devastating halter dress of rich, burgundy velvet, which exposed her back to the waist. The front was slit almost as deeply, but saving the dress from appearing brazen was a wide, antique-satin collar, framing the creamy expanse of skin between her breasts. She brushed her hair vigorously, allowing it to cascade down past her bare shoulders in waves reminiscent of the 1940's.

Ramsey had pulled out all the stops. The imported champagne flowed in such quantity that Noel noted that it had probably been eons since the desert community had been blessed with quite so much liquid. The elaborately decorated buffet tables draped in the colors of the network logo were laden with platters of roast ham, turkey and mountains of caviar.

The guest list included a lot of people in the industry, all of whom wished Noel the best of luck with only the slightest tinge of envy. She knew the odds for a chance like she'd been given. And, in a town that was built on gambling, people dreamed of the big payoff.

She was chatting with Beth Cochran, an old friend, when the other woman suddenly caught her breath.

"Don't turn around," she hissed, "but there is one absolutely gorgeous man looking this way!"

A tremor of alarm tingled up Noel's bare back, but she kept her voice perfectly calm. "Anyone we know?"

"I hear from the grapevine that you do. And I'd love to," the perky blonde stated, eyeing him with unabashed interest. Oh, he's coming over," she breathed excitedly. "Don't turn around!"

"I have to, silly," Noel hissed back. "Or how can I introduce you?"

"That's an excellent point," Beth affirmed, wrinkling her pert nose. "I guess it's just that cleverness that made you such a natural for the network. . . . Oh, hello," she gushed, smiling sweetly at a point somewhere above Noel's shoulder.

Noel turned slowly, raising her head instinctively to meet his vibrant, dark brown eyes.

"Hello, Ross," she greeted him softly. "I hadn't realized you were on the guest list."

"She always has this way of making me feel so welcome at parties," he drawled past her to the avidly interested Beth.

"Excuse me," Noel flustered. "Beth, Ross McCormick. Ross, Beth Cochran. Beth is the weekend news anchor over at KXYZ," she added, thinking there was no need to add Ross's occupation. Anyone who lived in this town and didn't recognize the name would have spent the last two years in hibernation.

"I know," he said, smiling warmly at Beth. "I always try to watch you when I'm in town. When I'm in bed suffering on Sunday night, all bruised after a game, I find you extraordinarily comforting."

The cheerful young woman grimaced prettily. "Just my luck. To discover I've a soothing effect on men like you," she teased. "That's not what I'd hoped for, Ross."

He laughed, seeming delighted with her frankness. "Now that I've met you in person, I'll be watching with an entirely new viewpoint."

"There you are, Beth." Ramsey broke into the conversation suddenly. "I've someone who's dying to meet you." He grinned conspiratorially at Noel, who had the strange feeling he'd just orchestrated Beth's kidnapping.

Beth put a hand on Ross's arm. "We'll discuss your new viewpoint sometime soon, I hope," she grinned provocatively, allowing Ramsey to lead her away.

"Nice party."

"Ramsey always throws wonderful parties," Noel agreed.

Ross gave her a dour glance. "You'd know about that better than I."

"I suppose I would."

"Congratulations on your new job. Now you're on the fast track to your anchor post. Everything you ever wanted."

He was facing her, but his eyes were focused somewhere distantly beyond her pale face.

"Thank you. I guess." She hadn't missed the barb in his tone.

Ross gave her the icy mimicry of a smile. "You're welcome. I'm sure you'll be just terrific."

Noel observed him closely, noticing for the first time the lines of strain on his face. "Thanks," she answered, letting her voice soften a bit. "I'm scared to death, actually."

She saw his broad shoulders slump. "I hate this conversation," he muttered.

"Perhaps I could locate Beth. You seemed to enjoy your little chat with her." Noel's voice was brittle.

His dark gaze speared her. "Don't talk like that. It doesn't suit you."

Noel sighed. "You're right. I don't like this conversation either. Why don't we just retire to neutral corners of the party?"

Ross moved swiftly, putting his hand firmly on the small of her back. His touch sent her senses clamoring, and she cursed her body inwardly for its answering response.

"I've got a better idea," he growled softly, leading her to the French doors that led outside.

"It's December. It's not warm enough to go outside."

His glance took in her bare back and he shrugged out of his midnight-blue dinner jacket, placing it about her shoulders. Noel inhaled the leather scent of his after-shave mingling with that familiar, heady male essence of him in the fibers and pulled the jacket tighter about her.

"When do you leave?" Ross asked abruptly, as soon as they were alone.

"I don't know, exactly," she confessed. "Right now it looks like I leave when you lose. I'm supposed to be covering the Lobos' miracle season."

He jammed his hands into his pockets, his broad shoulders narrowed as if to glance off an impending blow. "Then, I'm in a no-win situation."

Noel looked up into his grim face. "What do you mean?"

"I mean," he grated, "that if the team keeps winning, I have to watch you every day. I have to watch everyone strutting around like a bunch of male peacocks in heat whenever you walk onto that field."

He reached out and touched her hair. The moon

was creeping through the trees, tangling in the branches, silvering the trunks and sending splinters of light to sparkle in the midnight depths of her hair.

"I have to remember to keep my hands from running down the silkiness of your hair. Touching the satin length of your throat with my lips," he continued in a low, husky voice, which grew harsher. "But, if we lose . . . then you go."

"It was your decision, Ross," Noel replied softly. "I don't remember being given much choice. Didn't you give some nice, pat little speech about life and fairness and everyone doing his own thing?"

The chiseled features of his face were hard and implacable. "For a woman known for her independent attitude, you sure picked a dandy time to let someone tell you what to do."

It was an intriguing idea that Ross McCormick seemed as confused by all of this as she was. Was he now wishing she'd refused to leave his apartment that day? Turned down the network offer? When were they going to stop all this shadowboxing and really determine where they stood?

"May I ask a question?"

"You're the news lady."

Noel looked up at him with eyes that spangled with tears. "Why are we fighting like this?"

His black eyes were half-sheathed by heavy lids as he observed her gravely. Noel was only given a moment's warning before the warmth of his mouth covered hers. She knew she should remain cold and distant, denying the desire he was creating with the searching devastation of his kiss. He'd already hurt her badly. And giving in again could only deepen her pain. Yet, her own lips had been starving for the feel of his mouth, and her hands flung about his neck as she answered the sweet demands of his kiss.

Her movements caused his jacket to fall to the brick terrace floor, but neither noticed as his lips scorched a trail down her throat, causing her to moan softly. His hands moved across her back, heating the night-cooled flesh. Noel gasped with delight as they slid into the waistband of her dress and pressed her tightly against the hard line of his hipbone.

The feathering of his ragged breath filled her mouth with warmth as he repeated her name over and over. "Noel . . . oh, Noel. Come home with me."

"Oh yes," she breathed almost reverently, her hands skimming down his back as she leaned into him. "Yes, Ross."

He lifted his head, his features softening as he observed her love-flushed face. Her full, tenderly shaped mouth was soft and tremulous and all pretense had fallen from her slumberous jade eyes. Noel could feel the trembling of his long fingers as he traced the line of her jaw, and she knew that Ross was as incapable as she of closing the floodgates.

"Do you have a coat?"

"Leave it," she murmured, feeling dazed by the throbbing beat in her inflamed veins. "Ramsey will take care of it."

"You'll catch cold."

She put her hand on the hard, muscular arm. "Really, Ross, I'm warm. Your jacket is fine." The feel of the strong arm under her fingertips sent a shiver up her like quicksilver, and his eyes narrowed, catching the tremor.

"You're not wearing it anymore," he observed with a crooked smile.

Noel's dazed eyes followed his to the dark red bricks and watched as he bent down and picked up the forgotten jacket.

"It's not very stylish," he murmured, placing it back around her shoulders. "Are you certain you don't want me to go in and retrieve your coat?"

She shook her dark, glossy head, her hair swirling between them like a cloud. "No." Her speech was blurred with desire as she looked up at him. "Don't leave me, Ross. This is fine. Just take me home. Please. I've missed you so much."

Ross crushed her against him for a brief, shuddering embrace, and as his cheek rested on her hair, the angle kept Noel from observing the suspicious sheen that was glistening in his dark brown eyes.

"Me, too, babe." The words emerged on a groan. "Let's get out of here."

As he walked her to the black Porsche, Noel's dazed mind tried to make some sense of what she was about to do. What difference would it make? She was still going to Houston. He was still remaining behind in Las Vegas. That fact, which had been hovering between them spoiling things since her return from New York, would not be expunged.

So why was she doing this?

Because she'd die if she didn't.

Noel was unaware of the actions they took to leave the car and arrive in her bedroom, but once there, their eager hands made short work of their clothing.

"God, Noel, I'd forgotten how beautiful you are." Ross's dark eyes blazed with unsatiated hunger as he lay beside her, his fingers trailing along her bare flesh, tracing every curve.

"I haven't forgotten," she whispered, her own exploring hands sliding over the rippled muscles of his chest. "I remember everything."

"I lied," Ross murmured, capturing her nipples one

at a time between his thumb and forefinger and twisting in a sensual, teasing motion. The gesture brought waves of warmth flowing from Noel's feminine center as she struggled to concentrate on his soft, crooning words.

"About what?" she gasped, as the copper head gleamed against the smooth ivory of her skin, his lips tugging at the hardened pink crest of her breast. The deep sucking action caused her to cry out. "My God, Ross! Don't do that!"

The tawny head lifted, eyes brimming with a lazy heat. "You don't like it?" Ross asked innocently. His slanted grin that graced his flaming beard reminded her so much of the laughing, loving Ross McCormick who'd been absent from her bed for too long.

His palm just barely skimmed the ravished breast, and Noel arched her spine toward the teasing hand in desperate response.

"I love it," she admitted in a breathless sigh.

"Good. So do I."

The dark eyes flashed satisfaction as his head lowered to begin the agonizing seduction once again. "I didn't forget anything either," he murmured, finally answering her.

Her own hands were not idle, dancing over his body, inciting him to greater intimacies as she touched him without restraint. She heard his harsh intake of breath and felt the rapid beat of his heart as she slipped from his embrace to her knees, leaning over him, her long hair brushing the warm, moist skin, her lips raining a shower of kisses across his chest and stomach.

"Noel!" It was only her name, but it was a desperate prayer that escaped his throat as her tongue explored the hollow of his navel, jabbing, then licking with tender strokes. Her kisses blazed a trail down across his hard, flat belly, torturing and teasing him, her tongue tasting his skin as if she were sampling the ripest of fruits.

The raw urgency of Ross's need, so evident as he moved under her, served to fuel her own passions and she felt hotly alive, aflame with desire.

By the time her caressing, tasting tongue had explored every inch of him, Ross had reached the point of no return. His arms were like bands of steel—no, threads of silk, she decided—as they wrapped around her, rolling her onto her back. He hovered above her, his hair-brushed legs parting her satiny thighs; he treated her as if she were a delicate piece of crystal and not a woman who'd just driven him to the brink of agony.

Noel's hips strained up to reach him; the melt of her thighs met his as completion of the rapturous union introduced a delirium that was more earth-shattering than anything she'd ever experienced.

Before she'd known the joyous passion of Ross McCormick's lovemaking, Noel hadn't missed it, but once she'd learned the delight he could bring to her, her body had ached with a constant sense of loss. A loss he was filling now with his elemental male strength that had her sinking into the soft mattress, even as her hands clutched at him, pulling him deeper and deeper into her feminine warmth.

"Oh, Noel, I can't wait any longer," he groaned against her mouth, his teeth nibbling her full lower lip, his hot breath mingling with hers.

"Oh, Ross, don't wait. Please . . . love me, darling."

Noel and Ross were helpless in the grip of the dark whirling storm they'd created. They were caught up in the vortex of primitive desires as their bodies took over, erasing doubts and fears their minds might have used as barriers to total fulfillment.

Just as the primal force surged through her veins, followed by the cresting, heated waves, Noel felt the deep shudder of the man against her. Despite her intense joy, or perhaps because of it, huge tears began to flow in streams down her cheeks, dampening the love-moist skin of the man she loved.

Ross seemed to understand and murmured reassuring words as he kissed the tears away, rocking her in his arms as if sharing in her tumultuous emotions.

"I can feel your pulse." His lips brushed against the hollow of her throat, the dark russet-gold beard whispering against her skin.

"I'm surprised it hasn't leaped out of my body." Noel was basking in the heat of his body, enjoying the feel of his long legs still wrapped around her.

"Remember when you said we should break it off so neither one of us would get hurt?" she asked, her fingers playing idly with his thick hair.

"I remember."

"I did get hurt. What happened to your neat little plan, Ross?" Her eyes were glazed with a new supply of tears as she tried to hold his gaze to hers. But he appeared as nothing but a misty blur and she looked away.

"Two things. You got that assignment that waved you under my nose every day. And I discovered I'm lousy at playing a tough guy."

"You could have fooled me," she whispered falteringly. "You've practically left the field every time I showed up. Rob Fletcher was beginning to think we were supposed to be covering the NFL's phantom quarterback." Her voice cracked and she buried her face in his shoulder.

"Look, honey. This is difficult enough. I want to be with you. I've hated every minute we've been apart. I've missed you like crazy!"

"Do you have any suggestions?" Her wide hazel eyes searched his face, seeking a positive sign.

"Just one. Let's make the most of what we've got, instead of crying about what we can't have. I want to be with you every minute I can while you're still in town. I want to make love to you every night and fall asleep holding you in my arms. And wake up to you in the morning."

"And when the team loses?" Noel swallowed hard on the lump in her throat, a sob catching her words.

"Hey"—his fingers smoothed over the furrowed lines of her brow—"this is the old miracle quarterback here. Maybe I'll have an undefeated season."

Noel watched the fine network at the corners of his dark eyes deepen, his lips curving into a smile that encouraged an answering smile of her own. But much as Noel hated to deny this man anything, she couldn't muster up even a weak attempt.

"But if you don't? What then, Ross?"

"You go off to Houston. And we'll both have memories of a wonderful time in our lives. That isn't all bad, Noel."

No. It wasn't bad. But it certainly wasn't all that good, either! Was it so wrong? To want love—and a career?

Where was this perfect world she kept reading about in magazines? Inhabited by wonder women who were getting it all? And what yellow brick road did a person have to follow to get there?

12

The Lobos' next game was being played on a Monday evening, for television. Noel tried to tell herself that it was just another football game. But it was so much more. The outcome of the game would determine whether she was packing her clothes and heading immediately to Houston, or staying to follow Ross and the team through another grueling week. It seemed so unfair that somehow, once again, her life was tied to a damned game! Just how had she managed to lose control of her life? When she'd lost her heart to Ross McCormick, she answered her own question.

"You're going to get sick," she commented dryly, looking down at the pile of peanut shells lying around Rob's feet. He'd been cracking them continuously since they'd arrived at the stadium, leaving little trails of discarded shells, like Hansel and Gretel in the witch's forest, while they covered the game.

"My mother always used to say that, too," he informed her cheerily, sweeping the minicam downfield as he followed the action.

"And?"

"And, it never happened. Dad used to swear I had a hollow leg."

"I wouldn't doubt it," Noel muttered, taking a long breath on her cigarette. It had been a seesaw, high-scoring game, and as they went into sudden-death overtime, the pressure was beginning to get to her.

"It's a lot better than those cigarettes," he commented, cracking another speckled brown nut.

"They don't make me fat. And I only smoke when I'm nervous," she argued.

"Terrific. So you'll be the skinniest patient in the cancer ward," he quipped. "And if you only smoke when you're nervous, we need to discuss our relationship. Since you've been puffing away like a chimney since I've known you, it must be me."

"No. You're not the cause."

"Aha," he suggested, his attention still directed to the bruising action on the playing field. "Could it be our noble gladiator, Ross McCormick?"

"That's unfair!" Noel flared at him, lowering her voice as she saw heads swivel toward them. "You've been listening to locker-room gossip."

"That's right. And I think you're crazy."

"Why?"

Rob lowered the minicam for a moment, turning to observe her soberly. "You haven't been eating," he pointed out. "You're chain-smoking; you've got circles under your eyes that even makeup can't hide. I say marry the guy and get it over with."

"You might be right," she agreed. "Except for just one small little detail you've overlooked."

"And what's that?"

"The man hasn't asked."

He gave her a long, steady look before hoisting his minicam back to his shoulder. "For a supposedly modern, liberated lady, Noel Heywood, you've got some prehistoric ideas. You wait for that guy to carry you off like some caveman and you might be waiting too long. Like forever."

Lost in troubled thought, Noel wasn't aware she'd also lost track of the game's progress until she heard Rob mumble, "Well, it looks like we pack."

Glancing up quickly, she saw the Chargers' kicker trotting out onto the field. A quick snap, a perfectly placed field-goal kick through the upright posts and the Lobos had dropped their first game of the season, 38-35. Rob was right. It was time to pack. Time to leave Las Vegas and begin her life again.

Noel wondered just how many opportunities for a fresh start she had left in her life. Surely a person couldn't keep escaping disasters by being handed a new life in a new city? Eventually, she'd have to stop running from her mistakes. But right now, contemplating Ross's grim expression as he headed for the locker room, Noel was glad she didn't have to begin putting that resolution into practice.

"Just a minute!" Noel took one desperate look at the half-packed carton of books, then raced to the door, scrambling over piles of her scattered possessions. Flinging open the door, she could only stare in surprise at the immense frame filling the space.

"Ross! I thought it was the movers," she stammered.

He gazed down at her, his face unreadable. "Disappointed?"

"Oh no," she breathed, "but what are you doing here?"

He moved past her into the apartment and began taking the books from the shelf and stacking them in the carton, adjusting the ones she'd thrown in in her haste. He looked up at her from his squatting position beside the box and said, "At this moment, I'm helping you pack."

She wasn't going to argue. Even now, when his very presence was certain to widen the gaping tear in her heart, Noel still wanted to be with him. Any way she could. For as long as she could.

"I could use the help," she said softly. "Thank you."

He moved quickly through the stacks of her belongings, swiftly efficient at packing as he seemed to be at everything else. She was grateful they were kept so busy. It kept conversation to a minimum as they worked quietly beside one another.

Finally, Noel breathed a sigh of relief when the stacks and mounds had been packed away into cartons and the boxes labeled.

"Coffee?" she asked, heading for the kitchen.

"Great," Ross agreed, lowering his long frame to the carpeting.

It was only once she was in the kitchen that she remembered. "Uh, Ross . . . ?"

"You've packed the coffee and the pot," he guessed correctly.

"I forgot to leave anything out!" Noel wailed in confirmation.

"That's okay." He patted the soft cream carpeting beside him. "Come rest for a while. You've earned it."

"You, too," she allowed as she sat next to him, her legs tucked to the side under her. Noel was intensely aware of his presence, her mind spinning back to another time they'd been together, there on her floor.

She struggled to keep the nervous strain from her voice.

"I really appreciate your help. I don't know how I could have gotten it all packed in time by myself."

His eyes scanned the contours of her face appraisingly. "Oh, I think you could do just about anything you set your mind to, Noel. And the moving men would have helped."

"But I promised them I'd have everything ready," she explained. "I don't think they'd have been overjoyed to face the mess you did earlier."

She'd pulled her long chestnut hair back from her face with a crimson scarf and his hand reached out, tugging lightly at one end, to slide it off. The quick gesture allowed her hair to tumble loose, full and free.

"I don't know," he murmured, his finger moving up and down her neck under the thick swathe of hair. "I think you could probably entice a man to do anything you wanted."

His deep, baritone voice was memorably husky and his tracing finger was sending electric shocks down the sensitive skin of her neck. Noel jumped up, stepping over boxes to reach her purse. Extracting a cigarette, she watched him warily through the spiral of thin smoke. She had to steel herself against the smooth seductiveness of the circumstance and the man, and she decided to turn and stand her ground.

"Haven't you done just about enough damage, Ross? Is that male ego you've got buried under all those layers of macho exterior so demanding that it needs my total destruction?"

He quirked a quizzical, copper eyebrow. "What do you mean?"

"First, you forced your way onto my program and almost ruined my career. Next, you charged your way into my life and nearly destroyed that, too. Now, when I'm trying my hardest to pick up the pieces, you show up to watch the total annihilation of Noel Heywood. Isn't that overkill? Didn't they teach you it's not good sportsmanship to run up the score when you've already ground your opponent into the field?"

Noel's legs were weak as she turned the full fury of her pain on him, and she slumped down onto a carton of kitchen utensils.

Ross's eyebrow dipped wildly for a moment, then resumed its natural full arch over the hooded depths of his eyes. "If I hadn't always admired the smooth gears turning about inside that pretty head of yours," he shot back, "I'd think you'd definitely flipped, Noel. Where did you get a notion like that?"

She refused to answer, and Ross spanned the space between them, crossing his arms over his chest, glaring down at her from his immense height. Daggers of lightning sparked from his dark, glowering eyes.

"Why don't you put out that cigarette so I'm not forced to look at you through a fog of suffocating smoke?"

Noel risked a glance upward, daring the bolts of lightning. "I believe this is still *my* apartment," she said bravely. "And I'll smoke in it if I choose to."

Ross continued his piercing glare, not budging an inch. Noel took one more shaky but defiant breath on the cigarette. Then she rose from the carton and crossed the room, jabbing the cigarette into an ashtray left forgotten on the counter.

"There! I did what you wanted! I *always* end up doing what you want. Does that make you happy?" Her eyes were sparkling with hot, angry tears.

His furious expression softened and he rubbed his eyes with a slow, tired gesture. "No," he muttered, "it doesn't. It never does anything but kill me to see you so unhappy."

Noel's legs almost buckled beneath her as the pain in his voice swept over her in black, suffocating waves. She leaned back against the counter, her hands gripping the Formica edge. Once again, she was experiencing the confusion that he was always able to provoke. But Ross didn't appear to be his authoritative self, either. It seemed as if her leaving was turning out to be just as hard on him.

"Ross?" There was a gentle pleading in her voice. She couldn't let it end this way. Wouldn't! She moved quickly to his side, her eyes rounded with distress. Her tongue nervously ran over her bottom lip as she looked up into his shuttered face and said softly, "You were wrong."

"I don't doubt it. About what?"

"Your plan. It still hurts."

There was dark regret shadowing his brown eyes, and Noel knew it was only mirroring her own unhappiness. Her breath caught in her throat as something flickered in his dark eyes before his lips softened to lower to hers. And just as his warm lips brushed hers, the shudder that shook his body was proof to Noel he would miss her as horribly as she'd miss him. Her arms were encircling his neck to bring him closer when the bell rang stridently. Again. Then a third time.

"Hey! Ross McCormick. Boy, whatta surprise!" The short, bulky man's face was wreathed in a wide grin of recognition. "Hey, Murray," he called to his partner still out in the hallway, "guess who's here? Ross McCormick!"

"Ross! Geeze." The tall blond man entered the apartment, extending his huge bear paw of a hand toward Ross. "I never miss a Lobos game. Me and the kid go every week you're in town. Sorry about that loss the other day." The man called Murray was shaking Ross's hand with a wild, pumping motion.

"Yeah, that was a bad break," the shorter of the two agreed. "But we're still goin' to the Super Bowl, right, Ross?"

Ross gave Noel an apologetic glance before answering. "We're sure going to try, fellas," he promised.

"You'll make it, Ross. We're countin' on you!" Murray turned to Noel, as if suddenly noticing her presence in the room and remembering his reason for being there. "Well, little lady, you all set?"

She flinched at the mover's choice of words, refusing to meet Ross's glance, which despite everything she knew would be amused. "Yes," she stated, "all this can go."

Murray rolled up his sleeves above the elbows, his arms long and brawny, one biceps emblazoned with a tattoo of a heart inscribed to "Marilyn." Noel wondered idly if Marilyn were his wife. Or was his wife another woman, forced to live with this vivid magenta reminder of a girl friend past?

"Come on, Joe," he ordered his partner. "We need to get this rig loaded before next year."

Ross turned to Noel. "I think I'm in the way here."

"Oh no," she protested quickly, her hand going to his arm.

"Hey, lady, you want the clothes to go, too?" Joe had reentered the living room carrying her suitcases and garment bag.

"No," she said, rescuing them from him. She knew there would be no chance for conversation now. And Ross knew it, too.

"There's one thing you've forgotten," he said softly, standing with her in the doorway.

"And what's that?"

"This is not your average dumb jock here. If I can

wade my way through those dull law books, I should be able to read a map and find my way to Houston." A ghost of a smile hovered about the firm mouth nestled in the flaming beard. "When we play there, may I see you?"

Noel could feel the tears pricking at the back of her eyes, but she forced a slight, wobbly smile. "Not only can you see me," she said softly, with a trace of humor reasserting itself to ease their parting. "But I'm warning you, be prepared to be held hostage for a very long time."

"Now that's just a chance I'll have to take." He sighed heavily and lowered his mouth to hers, searching the tender corners of her mouth with his plunging tongue, kissing her with a thoroughness they both knew would have to sustain them for far too long.

Noel reached up, grasping his head in both hands, her heart lurching at the burst of desire brought about by the cataclysmic force of the kiss. Her mouth clung to his, acquiescing to his insistent demands, inviting the heated compulsion to continue. He searched the dark, moist interior of her mouth passionately, but Noel knew that it was not she who was the cause of his tormented frustration. It was circumstance; that twisting, inexplicable fate that had thrown them together then hurled them apart.

She was as desperate as Ross, crying out with a soft whimper as he dragged his mouth from hers to enable them both to inhale deep breaths of life-giving air. He turned his lips into her hair.

"Good-bye, Noel. Take care. And, honey—"

"Yes?" Her voice cracked.

"If you don't want to see me when I come, I'll understand."

"Don't even suggest such a thing," she threatened, emerald eyes glazed with a moist sheen, "or I'll go on the air and tell every opposing lineman in the country your weakness!"

"And that is? Besides you, of course."

Her lips trembled, making the forced smile appear a strange, crooked thing. "That you're ticklish."

"A treacherous trick"—he shook his brilliant, russet head—"but the wench never did play fair."

Noel watched from the balcony, scrubbing away at the free-falling tears with her knuckles as he took the inevitable yellow ticket from the windshield of his Porsche and shoved it deep into the pockets of his dark blue slacks. A sense of defeat washed over her as the low-slung car slid away, and she watched for a while as Murray and Joe loaded everything into their bright orange and black van. Everything except the one thing she needed. And he was remaining behind in Las Vegas.

The network had moved her into the offices of the Houston affiliate during the experimental stages of its new project, and Noel was relieved when she was made to feel welcome. While the tempo and excitement of booming growth made the city move to a steady, throbbing beat, the people were friendly and open. Few of the men in the work force wore ties and, at her station, everyone called each other by his or her first name, regardless of title.

Democracy also reigned supreme in the parking lot, where the early birds got the spots closest to the doors. Noel wondered somewhat sadly if Ross would find the casualness of Houston parking more to his liking. She knew that even if every third parking space in metropolitan Houston were reserved specifically for him, he'd still park illegally in one he felt suited his purposes just a little bit better.

The skyline of the city was in a state of constant flux

with buildings in various stages of completion, and it seemed as if Houston were bound and determined to keep up with the booming population.

"Just think," Rob remarked dryly as he helped Noel move into a spanking-new apartment complex flanked on either side by buildings under construction, "how nice this town will look when they get it finished."

Noel enjoyed the city, enjoyed the people and loved her new job. But there was a pall over her days. And it didn't take a Rhodes scholar to determine just what her problem was. She missed Ross. Pure and simple. But not so simple at all. Because there was no simple solution.

The network executives seemed pleased with her work; she'd received a number of complimentary memos. Ross seemed to have pegged the situation correctly. She was on the fast track now, moving straight up. But alone. And, suddenly, alone had changed into lonely. And the pot at the end of her rainbow seemed to be filled with fool's gold.

As the day approached for Ross to arrive at the Astrodome, Noel made her decision. Nothing was worth losing Ross. She would quit her job and return to Las Vegas with him. And if he didn't ask her to marry him, she would just have to ask him. They'd wasted too much time as it was.

She wouldn't go to the game; she was too frightened to wait outside the locker room. Watching the women hoping for a chance to meet the famous quarterback would bring back memories that might ruin their reunion. Noel didn't want to spend a single moment in public with him. She'd been patient. Now she wanted the man all to herself.

She was at the studio on Sunday afternoon, working with a tape editor, trying to keep busy, when one of the reporters hurried in.

"Hey, Noel," he said, "you know Ross McCormick, don't you?"

"Uh-hum," she answered, her eyes still on the moving images. Working hard to keep her composure, she was not about to discuss Ross with a virtual stranger.

"Then you'll probably be interested in my lead-in," he commented, going over to a desk to begin typing. The clacking of the old Underwood as he sped along with his index fingers almost drowned out his next words.

"What did you say?" she asked, one hand flying to her throat, where she could feel the wild tempo of her pulse under her fingertips.

"I said, he was running an option play when he got hit. He's unconscious."

"Where?" Everyone turned to look at Noel as she screeched her question and grabbed the man's arm to stop the incessant racket of the manual typewriter's keys.

He looked up into her blanched face, startled by her sudden, intense reaction. "They took him to the Texas Medical Center," he replied, then added, "It's right across Beaumont Highway from the Astrodome."

Noel grabbed her purse and ran toward the door.

"Hey!" the tape editor yelled after her. "What am I supposed to do with this tape?"

She didn't even bother to answer. The least of her concerns at that moment was the new koala bear born at the Children's Zoo.

13

The traffic was terrible, and Noel found herself in a stop-and-start snarl as thousands of fans left the game. Once inside the doors of the Texas Medical Center, she slowed her pace to a brisk walk, attempting to assemble an air of authority so she could determine just where they were hiding Ross.

"Oh yes, Mr. McCormick, the football player." The gray-haired matron at the admittance desk sniffed. Her attitude was definitely a contrast to her sunshine-yellow smock. "And may I inquire, just who—exactly—are you?"

"I'm his wife," Noel answered spontaneously. She was afraid that if she told the truth, this guardian of the door might refuse her admittance.

She'd charmed the dragon with the magic word. "Oh, I'm sorry, Mrs. McCormick." The woman was immediately apologetic, her smile no longer condescending. "You've no idea what a bother the press has been about all this. It's just ruined my entire day."

"My husband?" Noel prompted, hoping to forestall the narrative before it became too rambling.

"He's fine," she assured Noel. "The doctor says that except for a headache, he'll be fine. If you'll just follow me . . ."

Noel obediently followed the woman, whose rubber soles made a slight squeaking sound on the highly polished tile floor.

"Your wife is here to see you," she announced with a smile before backing away and leaving Noel to face Ross alone.

"My wife?"

Noel grinned. "I was afraid they wouldn't let me in to see you. So I lied."

His head was bandaged above his pale face, but his eyes twinkled.

"That's a relief. I was afraid I'd been out so long I couldn't remember our honeymoon." His gaze caressed the body that his hands knew so intimately. "I'm certain I could never be that far gone."

Noel moved to his bedside and took his hand in hers. "I love you," she said simply.

"I know."

"You know? Is that all you have to say?"

"You want me to tell you I love you, too?"

Her fingers laced through his long, slender ones. "I think that would be nice. But only if you mean it."

"Of course I do. We wouldn't have had nearly the problem if I hadn't been out of my mind over you. As soon as I realized what you were feeling, I'd have discouraged your brazen behavior in my tactful, subtle manner. And you'd have been back in your comfy little television studio, all safe and sound. But I couldn't let you go." There was a deep note of contrition in the low velvet voice, and Noel knew they'd both suffered.

"Brazen?" she inquired softly, lifting a dark eyebrow.

"Of course. Don't you remember, wench, just who outran whom? I seem to recall being held to the carpet by a wanton seductress."

"Speaking of running, what were you doing running an option play?"

He gave her a breathtakingly boyish grin that caused her heart to swell in response. "Trying to impress my girl?"

She shook her head, gingerly touching his bandaged forehead. "Are you sure you're all right?"

"I'll be fine," he promised, taking her hand and kissing each of the fingertips tenderly. "I'll be back for next week's play-off game, and then, after we win that, the big one."

"You think you'll play in the Super Bowl this year?"

"I'd like to go out with that."

Noel looked at him in surprise. "You're retiring?"

"Yep."

"Then what will you do?" Her hazel eyes were soft and vulnerable.

"I was thinking about getting married," he said softly, "but it seems you've beaten me to the idea."

Noel refused to play coy. "I think it's a perfect idea," she agreed, running her fingertips along the soft growth of beard. "Then what have you planned to do? After getting married?"

His hand reached out to trace her slender curves, allowing her body to respond with instant remembrance to his touch.

"You need to ask that? I was already shocked into

thinking I'd missed one honeymoon. I'm not about to forgo this one."

There was nothing Noel wanted more than to be lying in the arms of this man, as his wife. She certainly wasn't marrying him because he could throw a football. Or because he was so wonderfully handsome. Or because the very touch of those talented hands could cause her entire body to melt. Well, perhaps a little bit for that reason. But there were so many others.

"I meant, after that," she prompted.

"I thought I'd come to Houston. So I could make love to my wife regularly. Isn't that the best way to keep a honeymoon from ending?" Ross was watching her carefully.

"Move here?"

"Don't they need lawyers in Texas, ma'am?" he drawled.

"Oh, Ross," Noel sighed happily. "I love you so much!"

"And I adore you, sweetheart." His voice lowered and Noel looked with concern at the furrows creasing his forehead beneath the stark white bandage. As she watched, she observed the cloudy film of pain cross his dark eyes.

"Does it hurt too much, darling?" she asked softly, longing to stroke his head, but afraid of causing more pain.

"A little," he admitted, "but it's not the first concussion I've received. Let's just hope it's the last."

Ross lay his head back upon the white pillow and closed his eyes. Noel looked at the thick lashes resting on the unusually wan face and saw a lush, red-gold fringe.

"Ross? Would you like me to leave now?"

"Honey," he breathed, his eyes still shut, "I don't

want you *ever* to leave me. But, could you straighten my pillow? Just a little?"

"Of course." Noel leaned forward, adjusting the pillow under his coppery, wrapped head, when suddenly his arms shot out and he pulled her down to him, his lips smothering her startled gasp.

Once the initial shock was past, Noel responded, her lips moving eagerly against his. It was a kiss of passion, but it was a kiss of promise, too. When she finally broke away for air, she scolded him lightly.

"You cheated," she complained. "I thought you were in pain."

Ross pulled her close to him, the familiar dancing light in the depths of his dark eyes. As his strong hands adjusted her slim body to fit against him in the narrow hospital bed, he laughed huskily, his breath fanning her skin as he rained kisses down her throat.

"My darling Noel," he whispered delightedly, "don't tell me an educated football expert like yourself has never heard of the quarterback sneak!"

Coming in October 1983
Janet Dailey

CALDER BORN CALDER BRED

The Calder family story which began so dramatically in <u>This Calder Sky</u> and continued in <u>This Calder Range</u> and <u>Stands A Calder Man</u> now comes to a close in this all-new novel, as powerful, as enthralling as the first three.

If you've thrilled to the first three Calder novels, you will not want to miss Janet Dailey's new novel—on sale in October.

Or, use the coupon below to order by mail
Pocket Books, Department 983
1230 Avenue of the Americas, New York, NY 10020
Please send me _____ copies of CALDER BORN, CALDER BRED (83610-2/$6.95). Please add 75¢ to cover postage and handling. NYS and NYC residents please add appropriate sales tax. Send check or money order—no cash, stamps, or CODs, please. Allow six weeks for delivery.

Name_____
Address_____
City_____ State/ZIP_____

Silhouette Desire

YOU'LL BE SWEPT AWAY WITH SILHOUETTE DESIRE

$1.75 each

- 1 ☐ CORPORATE AFFAIR James
- 2 ☐ LOVE'S SILVER WEB Monet
- 3 ☐ WISE FOLLY Clay
- 4 ☐ KISS AND TELL Carey
- 5 ☐ WHEN LAST WE LOVED Baker
- 6 ☐ A FRENCHMAN'S KISS Mallory
- 7 ☐ NOT EVEN FOR LOVE St. Claire
- 8 ☐ MAKE NO PROMISES Dee
- 9 ☐ MOMENT IN TIME Simms
- 10 ☐ WHENEVER I LOVE YOU Smith

$1.95 each

- 11 ☐ VELVET TOUCH James
- 12 ☐ THE COWBOY AND THE LADY Palmer
- 13 ☐ COME BACK, MY LOVE Wallace
- 14 ☐ BLANKET OF STARS Valley
- 15 ☐ SWEET BONDAGE Vernon
- 16 ☐ DREAM COME TRUE Major
- 17 ☐ OF PASSION BORN Simms
- 18 ☐ SECOND HARVEST Ross
- 19 ☐ LOVER IN PURSUIT James
- 20 ☐ KING OF DIAMONDS Allison
- 21 ☐ LOVE IN THE CHINA SEA Baker
- 22 ☐ BITTERSWEET IN BERN Durant
- 23 ☐ CONSTANT STRANGER Sunshine
- 24 ☐ SHARED MOMENTS Baxter
- 25 ☐ RENAISSANCE MAN James
- 26 ☐ SEPTEMBER MORNING Palmer
- 27 ☐ ON WINGS OF NIGHT Conrad
- 28 ☐ PASSIONATE JOURNEY Lovan
- 29 ☐ ENCHANTED DESERT Michelle
- 30 ☐ PAST FORGETTING Lind
- 31 ☐ RECKLESS PASSION James
- 32 ☐ YESTERDAY'S DREAMS Clay
- 33 ☐ PROMISE ME TOMORROW Powers
- 34 ☐ SNOW SPIRIT Milan
- 35 ☐ MEANT TO BE Major
- 36 ☐ FIRES OF MEMORY Summers
- 37 ☐ PRICE OF SURRENDER James
- 38 ☐ SWEET SERENITY Douglass
- 39 ☐ SHADOW OF BETRAYAL Monet
- 40 ☐ GENTLE CONQUEST Mallory
- 41 ☐ SEDUCTION BY DESIGN St. Claire
- 42 ☐ ASK ME NO SECRETS Stewart
- 43 ☐ A WILD, SWEET MAGIC Simms
- 44 ☐ HEART OVER MIND West
- 45 ☐ EXPERIMENT IN LOVE Clay
- 46 ☐ HER GOLDEN EYES Chance
- 47 ☐ SILVER PROMISES Michelle
- 48 ☐ DREAM OF THE WEST Powers
- 49 ☐ AFFAIR OF HONOR James
- 50 ☐ FRIENDS AND LOVERS Palmer
- 51 ☐ SHADOW OF THE MOUNTAIN Lind
- 52 ☐ EMBERS OF THE SUN Morgan

Silhouette Desire

- 53 ☐ WINTER LADY Joyce
- 54 ☐ IF EVER YOU NEED ME Fulford
- 55 ☐ TO TAME THE HUNTER James
- 56 ☐ FLIP SIDE OF YESTERDAY Douglass
- 57 ☐ NO PLACE FOR A WOMAN Michelle
- 58 ☐ ONE NIGHT'S DECEPTION Mallory
- 59 ☐ TIME STANDS STILL Powers
- 60 ☐ BETWEEN THE LINES Dennis
- 61 ☐ ALL THE NIGHT LONG Simms
- 62 ☐ PASSIONATE SILENCE Monet
- 63 ☐ SHARE YOUR TOMORROWS Dee
- 64 ☐ SONATINA Milan
- 65 ☐ RECKLESS VENTURE Allison
- 66 ☐ THE FIERCE GENTLENESS Langtry
- 67 ☐ GAMEMASTER James
- 68 ☐ SHADOW OF YESTERDAY Browning
- 69 ☐ PASSION'S PORTRAIT Carey
- 70 ☐ DINNER FOR TWO Victor
- 71 ☐ MAN OF THE HOUSE Joyce
- 72 ☐ NOBODY'S BABY Hart
- 73 ☐ A KISS REMEMBERED St. Claire
- 74 ☐ BEYOND FANTASY Douglass
- 75 ☐ CHASE THE CLOUDS McKenna
- 76 ☐ STORMY SERENADE Michelle
- 77 ☐ SUMMER THUNDER Lowell
- 78 ☐ BLUEPRINT FOR RAPTURE Barber
- 79 ☐ SO SWEET A MADNESS Simms
- 80 ☐ FIRE AND ICE Palmer
- 81 ☐ OPENING BID Kennedy
- 82 ☐ SUMMER SONG Clay
- 83 ☐ HOME AT LAST Chance
- 84 ☐ IN A MOMENT'S TIME Powers
- 85 ☐ THE SILVER SNARE James
- 86 ☐ NATIVE SEASON Malek
- 87 ☐ RECIPE FOR LOVE Michelle
- 88 ☐ WINGED VICTORY Trevor
- 89 ☐ TIME FOR TOMORROW Ross
- 90 ☐ WILD FLIGHT Roszel
- 91 ☐ IMAGE OF LOVE Browning
- 92 ☐ MOUNTAIN MEMORY Carey
- 93 ☐ SILENT BEGINNINGS Berk
- 94 ☐ WINNING SEASON Robbins
- 95 ☐ THE MARRYING KIND Summers
- 96 ☐ SUMMERSON Milan

SILHOUETTE DESIRE, Department SD/6
1230 Avenue of the Americas
New York, NY 10020

Please send me the books I have checked above. I am enclosing $_____
(please add 75¢ to the cover postage and handling. NYS and NYC residents please add appropriate sales tax.) Send check or money order—no cash or C.O.D.'s please. Allow six weeks for delivery.

NAME _____

ADDRESS _____

CITY _____ STATE/ZIP _____

Silhouette Desire 15-Day Trial Offer

A new romance series that explores contemporary relationships in exciting detail

Six Silhouette Desire romances, free for 15 days! We'll send you six new Silhouette Desire romances to look over for 15 days, absolutely free! If you decide not to keep the books, return them and owe nothing.

Six books a month, free home delivery. If you like Silhouette Desire romances as much as we think you will, keep them and return your payment with the invoice. Then we will send you six new books every month to preview, just as soon as they are published. You pay only for the books you decide to keep, and you never pay postage and handling.

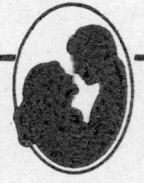

--- MAIL TODAY ---

Silhouette Desire, SDSD7U
120 Brighton Road, Clifton, NJ 07012

Please send me 6 Silhouette Desire romances to keep for 15 days, absolutely free. I understand I am not obligated to join the Silhouette Desire Book Club unless I decide to keep them.

Name_____

Address_____

City_____

State_____ Zip_____

This offer expires June 30, 1984

Love, passion and adventure will be yours FREE for 15 days... with Tapestry™ historical romances!

"Long before women could read and write, tapestries were used to record events and stories... especially the exploits of courageous knights and their ladies."

And now there's a new kind of tapestry...

In the pages of Tapestry™ romance novels, you'll find love, intrigue, and historical touches that really make the stories come alive!

You'll meet brave Guyon d'Arcy, a Norman knight... handsome Comte Andre de Crillon, a Huguenot royalist... rugged Branch Taggart, a feuding American rancher... and more. And on each journey back in time, you'll experience tender romance and searing passion... and learn about the way people lived and loved in earlier times than ours.

We think you'll be so delighted with Tapestry romances, you won't want to miss a single one! We'd like to send you 2 books each month, as soon as they are published, through our Tapestry Home Subscription Service.℠ Look them over for 15 days, free. If not delighted, simply return them and owe nothing. But if you enjoy them as much as we think you will, pay the invoice enclosed. There's never any additional charge for this convenient service—we pay all postage and handling costs.

To receive your Tapestry historical romances, fill out the coupon below and mail it to us today. You're on your way to all the love, passion, and adventure of times gone by!

HISTORICAL *Tapestry* ROMANCES

Tapestry Home Subscription Service, Dept. TPSD09
120 Brighton Road, Box 5020, Clifton, NJ 07012

Yes, I'd like to receive 2 exciting Tapestry historical romances each month as soon as they are published. The books are mine to examine for 15 days, free. If not delighted, I can return them and owe nothing. There is never a charge for this convenient home delivery—no postage, handling, or any other hidden charges. If I decide to keep the books, I will pay the invoice enclosed.

I understand there is no minimum number of books I must buy, and that I can cancel this arrangement at any time.

Name _____

Address _____

City _____ State _____ Zip _____

Signature _____ (If under 18, parent or guardian must sign.)

This offer expires January 31, 1984.

Tapestry™ is a trademark of Simon & Schuster.

READERS' COMMENTS ON SILHOUETTE DESIRES

"Thank you for Silhouette Desires. They are the best thing that has happened to the bookshelves in a long time."
—V.W.*, Knoxville, TN

"Silhouette Desires—wonderful, fantastic—the best romance around."
—H.T.*, Margate, N.J.

"As a writer as well as a reader of romantic fiction, I found DESIREs most refreshingly realistic—and definitely as magical as the love captured on their pages."
—C.M.*, Silver Lake, N.Y.

*names available on request